SOUTH HOLLAND PUBLIC LIBRARY

3 1350 00300 6709

W9-AYE-801

DISCARD

South Holland Public Library
South Holland, Illinois

DISCARD

GAYLORD

OPPOSING
VIEWPOINTS®
SERIES

Religion in America

Other Books of Related Interest:

Opposing Viewpoints Series
Abortion
The Catholic Church
Ethics
Human Rights

Current Controversies Series
The Human Genome
Medical Ethics

At Issue Series
The Ethics of Capital Punishment
How Does Religion Influence Politics?
Should Character Be Taught in School?
Women in Islam

"Congress shall make no law . . . abridging the freedom of speech, or of the press."

First Amendment to the U.S. Constitution

The basic foundation of our democracy is the First Amendment guarantee of freedom of expression. The Opposing Viewpoints Series is dedicated to the concept of this basic freedom and the idea that it is more important to practice it than to enshrine it.

Religion in America

David Haugen and Susan Musser, Book Editors

GREENHAVEN PRESS
A part of Gale, Cengage Learning

GALE
CENGAGE Learning™

Detroit • New York • San Francisco • New Haven, Conn • Waterville, Maine • London

SOUTH HOLLAND PUBLIC LIBRARY

GALE
CENGAGE Learning™

Christine Nasso, *Publisher*
Elizabeth Des Chenes, *Managing Editor*

© 2011 Greenhaven Press, a part of Gale, Cengage Learning

Gale and Greenhaven Press are registered trademarks used herein under license.

For more information, contact:
Greenhaven Press
27500 Drake Rd.
Farmington Hills, MI 48331-3535
Or you can visit our Internet site at gale.cengage.com

ALL RIGHTS RESERVED.
No part of this work covered by the copyright herein may be reproduced, transmitted, stored, or used in any form or by any means graphic, electronic, or mechanical, including but not limited to photocopying, recording, scanning, digitizing, taping, Web distribution, information networks, or information storage and retrieval systems, except as permitted under Section 107 or 108 of the 1976 United States Copyright Act, without the prior written permission of the publisher.

For product information and technology assistance, contact us at

Gale Customer Support, 1-800-877-4253
For permission to use material from this text or product, submit all requests online at www.cengage.com/permissions

Further permissions questions can be emailed to permissionrequest@cengage.com.

Articles in Greenhaven Press anthologies are often edited for length to meet page requirements. In addition, original titles of these works are changed to clearly present the main thesis and to explicitly indicate the author's opinion. Every effort is made to ensure that Greenhaven Press accurately reflects the original intent of the authors. Every effort has been made to trace the owners of copyrighted material.

Cover image copyright © iStockPhoto.com/McClister Photography.

LIBRARY OF CONGRESS CATALOGING-IN-PUBLICATION DATA

Religion in America / David Haugen and Susan Musser, book editors.
     p. cm. -- (Opposing viewpoints)
   Includes bibliographical references and index.
   ISBN 978-0-7377-4988-5 (hardcover) -- ISBN 978-0-7377-4989-2 (pbk.)
   1. United States--Religion. I. Haugen, David M., 1969- II. Musser, Susan.
   BL2525.R4646 2010
   200.973--dc22
                                                                   2010016975

3 1350 00300 6709

Printed in the United States of America
1 2 3 4 5 6 7 14 13 12 11 10

Contents

Chapter 3: What Should Be Done to Accommodate Religious Freedom in America?

Chapter 4: What Values Should Religious Americans Support?

Why Consider
Opposing Viewpoints?

> *"The only way in which a human being can make some approach to knowing the whole of a subject is by hearing what can be said about it by persons of every variety of opinion and studying all modes in which it can be looked at by every character of mind. No wise man ever acquired his wisdom in any mode but this."*
>
> John Stuart Mill

In our media-intensive culture it is not difficult to find differing opinions. Thousands of newspapers and magazines and dozens of radio and television talk shows resound with differing points of view. The difficulty lies in deciding which opinion to agree with and which "experts" seem the most credible. The more inundated we become with differing opinions and claims, the more essential it is to hone critical reading and thinking skills to evaluate these ideas. Opposing Viewpoints books address this problem directly by presenting stimulating debates that can be used to enhance and teach these skills. The varied opinions contained in each book examine many different aspects of a single issue. While examining these conveniently edited opposing views, readers can develop critical thinking skills such as the ability to compare and contrast authors' credibility, facts, argumentation styles, use of persuasive techniques, and other stylistic tools. In short, the Opposing Viewpoints Series is an ideal way to attain the higher-level thinking and reading skills so essential in a culture of diverse and contradictory opinions.

In addition to providing a tool for critical thinking, Opposing Viewpoints books challenge readers to question their own strongly held opinions and assumptions. Most people form their opinions on the basis of upbringing, peer pressure, and personal, cultural, or professional bias. By reading carefully balanced opposing views, readers must directly confront new ideas as well as the opinions of those with whom they disagree. This is not to argue simplistically that everyone who reads opposing views will—or should—change his or her opinion. Instead, the series enhances readers' understanding of their own views by encouraging confrontation with opposing ideas. Careful examination of others' views can lead to the readers' understanding of the logical inconsistencies in their own opinions, perspective on why they hold an opinion, and the consideration of the possibility that their opinion requires further evaluation.

Evaluating Other Opinions

To ensure that this type of examination occurs, Opposing Viewpoints books present all types of opinions. Prominent spokespeople on different sides of each issue as well as well-known professionals from many disciplines challenge the reader. An additional goal of the series is to provide a forum for other, less known, or even unpopular viewpoints. The opinion of an ordinary person who has had to make the decision to cut off life support from a terminally ill relative, for example, may be just as valuable and provide just as much insight as a medical ethicist's professional opinion. The editors have two additional purposes in including these less known views. One, the editors encourage readers to respect others' opinions—even when not enhanced by professional credibility. It is only by reading or listening to and objectively evaluating others' ideas that one can determine whether they are worthy of consideration. Two, the inclusion of such viewpoints encourages the important critical thinking skill of objectively evaluating an author's credentials and bias. This evaluation will illuminate an author's reasons for taking a particular stance on an issue and will aid in readers' evaluation of the author's ideas.

It is our hope that these books will give readers a deeper understanding of the issues debated and an appreciation of the complexity of even seemingly simple issues when good and honest people disagree. This awareness is particularly important in a democratic society such as ours in which people enter into public debate to determine the common good. Those with whom one disagrees should not be regarded as enemies but rather as people whose views deserve careful examination and may shed light on one's own.

Thomas Jefferson once said that "difference of opinion leads to inquiry, and inquiry to truth." Jefferson, a broadly educated man, argued that "if a nation expects to be ignorant and free . . . it expects what never was and never will be." As individuals and as a nation, it is imperative that we consider the opinions of others and examine them with skill and discernment. The Opposing Viewpoints Series is intended to help readers achieve this goal.

David L. Bender and Bruno Leone,
Founders

Introduction

> "Thomas Jefferson and the other founders built our nation upon Christian principles and ethics, and warned that the United States would morally disintegrate if it forsook its "religious" roots. Although such a foundation could not make our nation "Christian," we would be wise to listen to our predecessors and embrace our Creator and the Bible that communicates how to walk in morality and virtue."
>
> —Reb Bradley,
> parenting counselor
> and best-selling author.

> "It goes without saying that the actual purpose and effects of injecting religious dogma into government are never to make people more virtuous or holy but rather to advance specific political agendas. Sometimes the agenda is to wrap the aura of religiosity and holiness around a particular political party or faction; sometimes it is to get the state to resolve a problem that is internal to a religion; and sometimes it is just to promote sectarian creeds to the public and show religious minorities who's the boss."
>
> —Jamie Raskin,
> Maryland state senator.

The American Religious Identification Survey (ARIS) of 2008 revealed that America is less of a Christian nation than it was in 1990, the first year the survey was conducted. According to the ARIS, 86 percent of Americans identified themselves as Christian in 1990, but only 76 percent did so in 2008. Judaism has also lost adherents over the nearly two decades of the survey's span, and only immigration accounts for the slight rise of other religions such as Islam and Buddhism. As the proportion of Christians and Jews declined, the number of Americans who identified themselves as atheist, agnostic, or having no religious affiliation grew over the time period from 8.2 percent to 15 percent. Coupled with those who choose not to indicate a religious preference, these statistics indicate that one out of every five Americans failed to align themselves with a recognized faith.

R. Albert Mohler Jr., the president of the Southern Baptist Theological Seminary—a prominent scholarly institution, found the results of this survey disturbing. In response, he posted a column on his personal Web site that acknowledges, "A remarkable culture shift has taken place around us. The most basic contours of American culture have been radically altered. The so-called Judeo-Christian consensus of the last millennium has given way to a post-modern, post-Christian, post-Western cultural crisis which threatens the very heart of our culture." To explain this transformation, Mohler claims: "The evidence is overwhelming. Moral relativism has so shaped the culture that the vast majority of Americans now see themselves as their own moral arbiter."

In Mohler's view, the rise of atheism and moral relativism is directly related to the secularization of a culture that wallows under the influence of everything from mass media to psycho-therapeutic fads. Mohler insists that true Christians are now a "cognitive minority" in the United States. "To confess the truths of God's Word in late twentieth-century America," he argues, "is to take on a counter-cultural posture; to stand against the stream and to press against the grain." Mohler is not alone in holding this conviction. Christian leaders as well as thinkers and scholars from other faiths have for years bemoaned the secularization of the United States even as the majority of Americans still claim religious affiliation. Rabbi David Wolpe of Los Angeles warns his fellow conservative Jews, "We dare not permit [Judaism] to turn into a fossilized faith or a sacrifice to the seductions of modernity." All, including Mohler, assert that a revitalization of religious institutions and a commitment to faith are needed to stem the spiritual recession.

Some observers, however, are not so distraught at the statistics revealed in surveys like the ARIS. Writing for the Huffington Post in April 2009, law professor Bruce Ledewitz points out that "only 15% of respondents in ARIS identified [themselves] as secular. That means that America is still a very religious country and even a very Christian one. Nor will that change any time soon." Ledewitz, though, worries that the growing secularization of the United States could be damaging to the nation because religion does instill certain wisdom in its adherents that is not ingrained in nonbelievers. "Secularists have an unwarranted confidence in themselves and in a new cultural formation," Ledewitz writes. "In contrast, I think raising children without religion is quite difficult." To Ledewitz, the loss of spiritual values—that recognize the frailty of human beings and their shortcomings, yet insist on personal and communal betterment—is not a cause for celebration, especially if secular values cannot instill future generations with similar precepts.

Jon Meacham, the editor of *Newsweek*, believes the decline of Christianity in the United States may be good for the country and for Christians. In his view, loosening the hold Christianity has had on politics and culture will bring the United States back in line with the "separation of church and state" ideal that the Founding Fathers envisioned and may help Christians by clearly separating their religious devotions from worldly concerns. He maintains:

As crucial as religion has been and is to the life of the nation, America's unifying force has never been a specific faith, but a commitment to freedom—not least freedom of conscience. At our best, we single religion out for neither particular help nor particular harm; we have historically treated faith-based arguments as one element among many in the republican sphere of debate and decision. The decline and fall of the modern religious right's notion of a Christian America creates a calmer political environment and, for many believers, may help open the way for a more theologically serious religious life.

Thus, instead of seeing the decline as pitting religious Americans against the mainstream culture, as Mohler asserts, Meacham contends that the culture at large is better served if politics and religion remain discrete, giving the spiritual elements of culture their own space to flourish.

As leaders like Mohler and Wolpe fear, however, the disjuncture between faith and what Wolpe describes as "the seductions of modernity" are of prime importance in a country that still bears "In God We Trust" on its coins and defines itself as "one nation under God" in its pledge of allegiance. Many religious leaders believe that the separation between church and state means that immorality rules in a land that sanctions abortion, tolerates homosexuality, accepts the presumed disintegration of the nuclear family, and worships materialism. Some politicians agree. Republican congressman Ron Paul of Texas has argued, "The notion of a rigid separation between church and state has no basis in either the text of the Constitution or the writings of our Founding Fathers. . . . The Founding Fathers envisioned a robustly Christian yet religiously tolerant America, with churches serving as vital institutions that would eclipse the state in importance. Throughout our nation's history, churches have done what no government can ever do, namely teach morality and civility." Without being able to bring that morality to bear on public issues, however, many admit that secularism will ultimately shape U.S. values.

In *Opposing Viewpoints: Religion in America,* several spokespersons for faith and religious morality resist the notion that the United States is doomed to secular interests. As the contentiousness of their positions on such controversial topics as abortion, same-sex marriage, and the place of religion in education illustrate, the cultural battleground is far from secured, and the voices of the faithful are certainly not silent. Their critics, though, are not mute either; for while some lament the decline of religious affiliation and religious values in America, others hope that broader concepts of tolerance and freedom will ensure that the nation safeguards personal liberties. In chapters that ask Is America a Religious Nation? What Effect Does Religion Have on American Society? What Should Be Done to Accommodate Religious Freedom in America? and What Values Should Religious Americans Support? expert commentators from various camps offer their opinions on relevant issues of the day and forecast how the United States' moral compass may be changing. These debates signal that religion is still a vital force in American culture and politics, bearing out the words Thomas Jefferson wrote on religious freedom in Virginia—"that all men shall be free to profess, and by argument to maintain, their opinions in matters of religion, and that the same shall in no wise diminish, enlarge, or affect their civil capacities."

CHAPTER 1

Is America a
Religious Nation?

Chapter Preface

Throughout the twentieth and twenty-first centuries western European societies have gradually become more secular, while the United States, in comparison, has remained a nation where religion plays a significant role in both the public and private lives of its citizens. Statistics from large-scale public surveys in both the United States and Europe confirm this divergence in values. The European Values Study reported in 2003 that only 21 percent of Europeans count religion as "very important" while the 2002 Pew Global Attitudes report found that 59 percent of Americans claimed religion "plays a very important role in their lives." Much of this difference in attitude is often attributed to "American exceptionalism," which, with regard to religion, promotes the idea that the unique characteristics of the United States have restricted the nation from moving forward in a natural progression to become a more secular society. However, this longstanding consensus has come into question recently with the popularization of the idea that the United States' retention of religiosity is in fact in accordance with most other nations, and western Europe's secularization is actually the exception.

The notion that the United States is "exceptional" dates back to *Democracy in America,* the seminal 1831 work written by French political historian and philosopher Alexis de Tocqueville. Following a visit to the United States in the early years of the nineteenth century, de Tocqueville concluded that the condition of social equality in the United States was creating a new political and social system unlike that in Europe. Citing religion in particular, the Frenchman observed a concurrent, harmonious existence of faith and politics that he claimed was absent in France and could result only from the unique circumstances in the United States. Throughout the coming decades, the idea of American exceptionalism stuck, serving as a rote and dismissive response to why western European society embraced the secular and U.S. society continued to cling to the religious.

More recently, however, the predominance of American exceptionalism as an explanation of U.S. religiosity has come under fire. During a 2005 roundtable discussion hosted by the Pew Forum on Religion & Public Life, Austrian-born sociologist and theologian Peter Berger argued that when attempting to explain the increasing secularization of Europe in comparison with the United States, the "mistaken idea" of American exceptionalism must be discarded. He stated, "Most of the world is fiercely religious, and the United States is a strongly religious society. Thus, the exception is not the United States, but rather the exception is Europe."

While religiosity in the United States continues to be high in comparison with Europe, debate within the country persists as to whether the United States in fact remains, or was even founded to be, a religious nation. In the following chapter, the authors examine religion in the United States and debate its role in the country's founding, whether its influence is holding steady or diminishing in modern U.S. society, and whether religious people experience discrimination for their beliefs.

> *"America at the epoch of the founding was a country awash in religious fervor."*

America Was Founded on Religious Principles

M. Stanton Evans

While many historians suggest that the United States' Founding Fathers maintained a secularist view when drafting the documents that set out the laws of the nation, M. Stanton Evans argues that this suggestion is wholly inaccurate. Evans contends that early U.S. leaders were highly dependent on their religious beliefs in patterning the concepts and morality that undergird U.S. political ideals. Citing the beliefs of individuals such as George Washington, Thomas Jefferson, and Benjamin Franklin among numerous others, Evans makes the case that these men were devoutly religious, and even this select few were often much less pious than many of the lesser known founders who played significant roles in the formation of the United States. The secularization of the founding, Evans maintains, has been the work of recent historians who are seeking to strip the United States of its religious beginnings. M. Stanton Evans is a conservative journalist and author of the book The Theme Is Freedom: Religion, Politics, and the American Tradition.

M. Stanton Evans, "Faith of Our Fathers," *American Spectator*, vol. 40, February 2007, pp. 22–26. Copyright © The American Spectator 2007. Reproduced by permission.

As you read, consider the following questions:

1. According to Evans, what concepts have guided the writing of the a priorist historical studies of religion in the United States?

2. What are some of the "expressly Christian" statements made by George Washington and cited by the author as evidence of the first president's Christian beliefs?

3. What four early leaders, often cited as "skeptics, theological liberals, or devotees of secularizing doctrine," does Evans identify as being devoutly Christian?

Among his other odd distinctions, [French philosopher] Jean-Jacques Rousseau might be considered the patron saint of modern historiography. He at any rate caught the spirit of it when he said, in a famous passage, "Let us begin by setting aside all the facts, because they do not affect the question."

This fact-free technique, used often by Rousseau, wowed the literati of Europe circa 1750 and made him the toast of Paris. It seems to have impressed a lot of other people since, as the same non-empirical method has been routinely wielded in many academic studies, from retrospectives of the Middle Ages to discussions of the Cold War. In countless books and essays, relevant facts have indeed been set aside—or baldly misstated—to support some view already held before the history writing started.

In few cases has this been more apparent than in historical treatments of religion in the life of our republic, with particular emphasis on the War of Independence and constitutional founding that followed. The guiding concepts of these a priorist studies have been intense hostility to religion, a concomitant wish to downplay its importance, and a determined effort to write our history in keeping with such notions.

The effects of this have gone beyond the realm of academic error, bad as that is, to help work enormous changes in the social order. In obedience to lessons allegedly taught in these irreligious histories, archly secularist views have been imparted, and measures taken, severely wrenching the lives and customs of our people. This has in turn led to angry conflict on a host of faith-related issues—abortion, euthanasia, homosexuality, marriage—that now so painfully divide us.

Legal Exclusion of Religion

In legal terms, the most obvious manifestation of the problem has been a series of federal court decrees barring religious value and observance from vast sectors of American life. Bible reading and prayer in the public schools, display of the Ten Commandments, Christmas manger scenes, and other expressions of faith in public settings have been stamped out as contrary to the wishes of our Founders. The legal pretext for these rulings is that tax support for such observance violates the clause in the First Amendment prohibiting an "establishment of religion" in official practice.

The locus classicus [frequently cited example] for this view is the statement of Supreme Court Justice Hugo Black in a 1947 decision. "The 'establishment of religion' clause of the First Amendment," said Black, "means at least this: Neither a state nor the Federal government can set up a church. Neither can pass laws which aid one religion, aid all religions, or prefer one religion over another. . . . No tax in any amount, large or small, can be levied to support any religious values or institutions, whatever they may be called, or whatever form they may adopt to teach or practice religion."

This dictate has been enforced with increasing rigor through the years and, despite anomalies in the process, Black's absolutist doctrine is now accepted as conventional wisdom on the subject. And where it isn't yet applied as stringently as some would like, the legal watchdogs of the American Civil

Liberties Union [ACLU] and such are ever alert to enforce its sanctions. Thus by relentless pressure are the words and symbols of traditional faith driven from our discourse.

The court decrees that have produced all this are closely linked to the Rousseauvian method, as these edicts—somewhat distinctively for legal rulings—are based on a purported history of our founding. As explained in discursive comments by Justices Wiley Rutledge and David Souter, among others, we have to do these things because that's the way the Founders set it up. These far-seeing statesmen, we're told, mandated a strict separation of church and state when they adopted the First Amendment, so we're obliged today to banish tax support for religious doctrine.

The main champions of this outlook, it's said, were James Madison and Thomas Jefferson, who worked to disestablish Virginia's Episcopal Church in the 1780s, then carried the battle to the national level with the First Amendment. In this telling, Jefferson, Madison, et al., were proto-ACLUers: rationalists and skeptics who wanted a purely secular system. Banning prayer from the schools and all the rest are in alleged fulfillment of their vision.

Washington's Christian Proclamations

Astonishing as it may seem, given the axiomatic status of such notions, all of this is absurdly false—Rousseauvian history at its worst, running amok and at full throttle. On any fair examination of our country's past, the Black-Rutledge-Souter-ACLU rendition is not only wrong, but an exact inversion of the record. From the religious views and practices of the founding era, to Madison and Jefferson in Virginia, to the adoption of the First Amendment, the Court's rulings on these matters, and the history they embody, have blithely set aside the facts to reach a pre-ordained conclusion.

While the proofs of this are many, among the simplest ways of grasping the truth of the matter is to consult the

Religion in State Constitutions

Although all the Revolutionary state constitutions of 1776 affirmed in one way or another the Enlightenment belief in religious freedom, most of them did not abandon their traditional role in religious matters. To be sure, the official establishment of the Church of England that existed in a half-dozen colonies was immediately eliminated in 1776–1777. But the Revolutionary constitutions of Maryland, South Carolina, and Georgia authorized their state legislatures to create in place of the Anglican Church a kind of multiple establishment of a variety of religious groups, using tax money to support "the Christian religion." Many of the state constitutions provided for religious tests for officeholders. Six states—New Hampshire, Connecticut, New Jersey, the two Carolinas, and Georgia—required officeholders to be Protestant. Maryland and Delaware said Christians. Pennsylvania and South Carolina officials had to believe in one God and in heaven and hell; Delaware required a belief in the Trinity. And Connecticut and Massachusetts continued their Congregational establishments into the second and third decades of the nineteenth century.

Gordon S. Wood, New York Review of Books, *June 8, 2006.*

views of leading politicians in the revolutionary-constitutional epoch. In this respect the obvious place to start is with George Washington, military hero of the War of Independence, presiding officer at the Constitutional Convention, and first president of the new republic. Far from being a secularist or skeptic, Washington throughout his public life was a staunch supporter of the view that religious piety was essential to the well-being of the country.

Washington's most notable comment to this effect—though by no means the only one—was his Farewell Address, wherein he stated that "reason and experience both forbid us to expect that national morality can prevail in exclusion of religious principle." In the course of a long career he backed this precept with many actions, including proclamations of Thanksgiving to God and support for tax assessments to advance religious teaching. As commander of our military forces, he made diligent efforts to provide the armies with chaplains and require attendance at religious service.

Washington's statements on these topics, be it noted, weren't merely religious in some indefinite sense but were expressly Christian. Among his messages to his troops, for instance, was this from 1776: "The blessing and protection of Heaven are at all times necessary, but especially so in times of public distress and danger. The general hopes and trusts that every officer and man will endeavor to live and act as becomes a Christian soldier, defending the dearest rights and liberties of his country."

And this from 1778: "The commander-in-chief directs that Divine service be performed every Sunday at 11 o'clock, in each brigade which has a Chaplain. . . . While we are duly performing the duty of good soldiers, we certainly ought not to be inattentive to the higher duties of religion. To the distinguished character of a patriot, it should be our highest glory to add the more distinguished character of a Christian." All of which looks a lot like religious advocacy in a tax-supported setting (though tax support for Washington's armies was admittedly meager).

The Whitewashing of Religion

Not too different from Washington's comments were those of his successor to the nation's highest office, John Adams of Massachusetts. Adams frequently expressed in both private and public statements the belief that political liberty required

27

religious virtue. As he wrote to his wife Abigail in 1775: "Statesmen may plan and speculate for liberty, but it is Religion and Morality alone which can establish the principles upon which freedom can securely stand. A patriot must be a religious man."

Adams would reinforce this view in public statements when he became the country's leader. Vide [see] his presidential proclamation of 1798, urging his fellow citizens to "acknowledge before God the manifold sins and transgressions with which we are justly chargeable . . . beseeching Him at the same time of His infinite grace, through the Redeemer of the world, freely to remit all offenses and to incline us by His holy spirit to . . . repentance and reformation." This Trinitarian message was issued from the highest office in the land within a decade after adoption of the First Amendment.

Jefferson, who followed Adams as chief executive, is much cited by the secularizers, as he held views in some respects congruent with their model. Even so, the fit isn't a very good one, as Jefferson repeatedly voiced his faith in a providential God, and likewise expressed the view that freedom depended on religion. "Can the liberties of a nation be secure," he asked, "when we have removed their only firm basis, a conviction in the minds of the people that these liberties are of the gift of God?" Or, as he put it on another occasion: "The God who gave us life gave us liberty at the same time; the hand of force may destroy, but cannot disjoin them."

Madison, Jefferson's political ally and successor in the White House, is likewise cited in the standard histories, as he did hold separationist views, up to a point and with provisos. Yet he was on all the evidence not a skeptic, but a believing Christian. He was, for instance, a protégé of the Calvinist John Witherspoon at Princeton, read theology with his mentor, and maintained his interest in the subject for years thereafter. Between 1772 and 1775, he undertook an extensive study of Scripture at Montpelier. His papers include notes on the Bible made at this period and a pocket booklet on *The Necessary Duty of Family Prayer, with Prayers for Their Use.*

These four early leaders have been cited, not only because they were among the most eminent Founders, but also because they are often depicted in the standard histories as skeptics, theological liberals, or devotees of secularizing doctrine. Without pursuing that aspect here—and there is more to be said about it—suffice it to note that, if these were the liberals, we can well imagine what things were like in more orthodox circles of the era.

And, indeed, if we examine some of the other Founders, we find their ranks so replete with Bible-believing Christians as to suggest that America at the epoch of the founding was a country awash in religious fervor. Space permits only a sampling, but even a cursory survey is enough to suggest the errors in the standard version. Moving roughly North to South along the coastline, following are a few case studies.

Awash in Religious Fervor

Samuel Adams of Massachusetts, the wily strategist of independence, was an old-fashioned Puritan who saw in America the makings of a "Christian Sparta" not unlike the city on a hill envisioned by his Bay State forebears. He was a moving spirit at the Continental Congress of [17]74 in favor of having chaplains lead the group in prayer, despite denominational disagreements. As he put it: "I am not a bigot. I can hear a prayer by a man of piety and virtue, who is at the same time a friend of his country."

Sam Adams was not only a Puritan but represented a state with an established, tax-supported church—one that would remain established for the next six decades. His staunchly Calvinist views were shared by others from Massachusetts, including Caleb Strong and Elbridge Gerry, both delegates to the constitutional convention and members of the Federal Congress. Things weren't very different in Connecticut—yet another Puritan state with yet another tax-supported church—where constitutional founders Roger Sherman and Oliver Ellsworth were mainstays of the Puritan-founded Congregational Church, and served in Congress also.

Sherman, one of the most important but also most neglected of the Founders, was as much an oldfangled Puritan as Sam Adams. He objected to traveling on Sunday, was a leader in the ecclesiastical doings of New Haven, and engaged in theological correspondence even while tending to his worldly obligations. One of his writings is entitled, *A Short Sermon on the Duty of Self-Examination Preparatory to Receiving the Lord's Supper*. He would later play a pivotal role in shaping the religion clauses of the First Amendment.

Religiosity in the Northeast

New York State was more heterodox [unorthodox] than New England, but even here the religious convictions and activities of the founding generation were impressive. John Jay, co-author of *The Federalist* and later Chief Justice under the Constitution, was a devout evangelical Christian of Huguenot extraction. Rufus King, formerly of Massachusetts, would become warden of New York City's Trinity Church. The formidable Alexander Hamilton—often depicted as a skeptic—was another believing Christian who would prove his faith in dramatic fashion.

Next door in New Jersey, religious zeal burned more hotly still, as this was the home of Witherspoon, a one-man Christian Coalition. A Presbyterian divine [theologian] from Scotland, Witherspoon was not only an influential preacher, but a member of the Continental Congress and signer of the Declaration of Independence. He was also President of Princeton, where Madison and many other political leaders were his students, and which at the era of the founding was a stronghold of Calvinist Christianity.

Less acclaimed than Witherspoon, but known for piety also, was his New Jersey colleague Elias Boudinot, a leader in the Continental Congress and in the new Congress under the Constitution. It was Boudinot who, in September 1789, moved that Congress go on the record "in returning to Almighty God their sincere thanks for the many blessings He poured down upon them." This resulted in an overwhelming vote in favor of a day of prayer and Thanksgiving—passed the day after the House approved the language of the First Amendment.

In Pennsylvania (and Delaware), the learned John Dickinson, pamphleteer of America's cause in its legal contests with Great Britain, was a devout Quaker, and in 1781 would deliver a tough official message warning against the threat of creeping irreligion. Upon retirement from public life, he pursued intensive biblical studies, with particular focus on the Book of Matthew. His Pennsylvania colleague James Wilson, arguably the foremost legal scholar of the era, was another evangelical Christian, who opined that the "will of God" was the supreme law of nations. Benjamin Rush, the surgeon general of the revolution, was a stalwart Calvinist who believed "the Bible must be the center of education."

In Maryland, there was small chance that irreligion would flourish, as this was the refuge of America's then small band of Catholics. Foremost among these was the remarkable Carroll family—Archbishop John, signer of the Declaration Charles, and constitutional delegate Daniel. The two political Carrolls, like others mentioned, were members of the Congress that approved the First Amendment.

Southern Christian Devotion

Moving southward to Virginia, we find still other staunch religionists holding office. Though portrayed in many histories as a hotbed of irreligion—and there had been instances in the earlier going among the Cavalier squirearchy—the Old Dominion in the late eighteenth century was Ground Zero for religious fervor. This resulted from the so-called Great Awakening led by the Presbyterian Samuel Davies and the Baptists captained by John Leland. Patrick Henry was, for instance, much influenced by Davies and a zealous Christian. Other famous Virginians such as Edmund Pendleton, Richard Bland, and Edmund Randolph were likewise known for their devotion to religious causes.

Such examples might be multiplied indefinitely, but a few other instances may be briefly cited by way of wrap-up. Looking strictly at delegates to the constitutional convention, we note that David Brearly of New Jersey was a delegate to the Episcopal Convention of 1786; Richard Bassett of Delaware, a strong supporter of Methodist Bishop Francis Asbury; Hugh Williamson of North Carolina, a former Presbyterian preacher; Charles Cotesworth Pinckney of South Carolina, the longtime president of the Charleston Bible Society; and William Few of Georgia, "a staunch believer in revealed religion"—to cite only a handful from a considerable roster.

Disregard for Founders' Beliefs

Of course, no such discussion can omit the case of Benjamin Franklin, with Jefferson the quintessential American enlightenment figure, and like Jefferson a Unitarian in doctrine. Yet it was Franklin who at the Constitutional Convention called for prayer to aid the drafters in their efforts, saying that, the longer he lived, the more he was convinced "God governs in the affairs of men." Cynics have suggested that the old philosopher was showboating, as he sometimes did, but his private papers tell us he was sincere in this avowal, reflecting as his personal credo that "there is one God who made all things" who "governs the world by his providence," and who was to be adored and worshiped.

Ironically, Franklin's motion was opposed by Hamilton, objecting that a sudden resort to prayer might suggest things were going badly. This has led some secularizers to conclude

Hamilton was the skeptic—the "least religious of the founders," in one version. Yet as a youthful member of the Continental Army, we're told, he was known for religious devotion, and as a mature politician, sought to found a "Christian constitutional society" in "support of the Christian religion." Most tellingly, in the fatal duel with Burr, as Hamilton wrote beforehand, he resolved not to fire his weapon, "as the scruples of a Christian have determined me to expose my own life to any extent rather than subject myself to the guilt of taking the life of another."

If Hamilton was the "least religious" of the Founders, what does this say about the rest? And, more to the point of the larger history, what's the likelihood that people holding such opinions would have decided to ban religion from the conduct of the nation's business? As may be shown in some detail, the secular history in this respect is still more mistaken than in its casual disregard of fact in treatments of the individual Founders.

DISCARD
SOUTH HOLLAND PUBLIC LIBRARY

| *"The Founders strove to emphasize that separation from England was an expression of human rights, rather than Divine Right."*

America Was Founded on Secular Principles

Jack Feerick

In the viewpoint that follows here, Jack Feerick reaffirms the notion that the United States' Founding Fathers carefully and intentionally ensured that the foundational documents of the nation did not mandate or affirm any one religion, thus creating a secular state. While the author admits that religion did play a role in the private lives of many of the Founders, he insists that these personal beliefs did not infringe on the decisions made by these men with regard to legislating the separation of church and state in the country's formative years. Feerick maintains that the ongoing impact of this wall of separation is evident in the continued religious tolerance and freedom experienced by members of churches of all denominations. Jack Feerick is a writer and cultural critic for the Web site Popdose.

Jack Feerick, "Faith in America," *Saturday Evening Post*, vol. 281, November–December 2009, pp. 44–51. Copyright © 2009 Saturday Evening Post Society. Reproduced by permission.

As you read, consider the following questions:

1. What are two of the Enlightenment ideals that Feerick claims the Founding Fathers believed?

2. As stated by Feerick, how does the Constitution address the subject of religion?

3. What does the author identify as the two purposes of the First Amendment to the U.S. Constitution?

Thomas Jefferson didn't mince words when he gave his view on religious freedom: "It does me no injury for my neighbor to say there are twenty gods or no God," he once wrote. "It neither picks no pocket nor breaks my leg."

Jefferson's no-skin-off-my-nose attitude is so thoroughly modern that it's hard to remember just how radical his view was in its day. Despite the fact that America was colonized partly by settlers looking to practice their beliefs without discrimination, the Founders still lived in a world where government-sanctioned and -supported religion was the norm, where differences of faith and conscience could lead to seizure of property, bodily harm, and worse. By guaranteeing freedom of worship as a basic Constitutional right for all Americans, Jefferson and the rest of the Framers were attempting something entirely new. Almost miraculous, in fact.

Protecting Faithful and Faithless

Consider that the Constitution and the Bill of Rights were written exclusively [for] white, male landowners (many of them slaveowners), most with ties to just one specific religion—more than 50 percent of the Founding Fathers were affiliated with the Episcopal church, according to some historians. Not exactly the diverse dream team you or I might have chosen to safeguard the religious freedom of a new nation.

But that's exactly what they did, and in the first lines of the First Amendment: "Congress shall make no law respecting an establishment of religion, or prohibiting the free exercise thereof . . ." Known forever after as the Establishment Clause, this pronouncement and the entire amendment has over time proven to be a versatile tool that does more than separate church and state. It protects America's faithful and faithless alike, providing both freedom of religion and freedom from it, as appropriate.

To be sure, the Founding Fathers couldn't foresee how their efforts would one day help to make America the most religiously diverse nation in the world, nor anticipate how the Establishment Clause would come into play on future issues, from the teaching of evolutionary theory in schools, to the displaying of the Ten Commandments in public buildings, to the constitutionality of the Pledge of Allegiance.

For more than 200 years, the balance between religious liberty and the rule of law has been constantly renegotiated. To understand how that balance has been maintained both then and now, we need to look back at the influences that shaped the Founders and the documents they created to serve their country and—ultimately—us.

Balancing Faith and Secularism

The traditional idea of the Founding Fathers as conventionally pious Christian gentlemen is a myth, of course. But neither were they actively hostile to religion. John Adams, to pick one, remained a regular churchgoer throughout his long life. Jefferson, meanwhile, was skeptical of religion, yet revered Jesus as a great moral philosopher, even assembling a personal edition of the New Testament with scissors and a glue-pot, retaining the ethical teachings of Christ while editing out the miracles. (You can see the Jefferson Bible today at the Smithsonian in Washington, D.C.)

The time was ripe for change. This was the Age of Enlightenment, when advances in the sciences forced philosophers to reconsider humanity's place in the universe. Educated men of the day, including Jefferson and other Founding Fathers, were attracted to Enlightenment ideals and beliefs, including Deism: the notion of a Creator whose existence could be deduced from His handiwork, but who took no active part in human affairs—God as absentee landlord.

Another Enlightenment ideal that exerted a powerful influence over the Framers was the social contract. "Social contract theory holds that government doesn't descend from on high, but from voluntary agreements among ordinary citizens," says Gary Kowalski, author of *Revolutionary Spirits*, an account of the philosophical foundations of the Constitution. This all but flew in the face of conventional wisdom, which held that government derived its authority from God, from the top down.

As if that wasn't enough to lay the ground for revolutionary change, there was also an upswell of religious devotion among the colonial populace, with Evangelicals preaching that all men are created equal, and that each person's value is determined not by social class, but by moral behavior. Sound familiar?

The Declaration of Independence, then, served not just as the founding document of the American Revolution, but as a balance of the influences of the Founders and the average citizen. It asserted our unalienable rights, endowed by our Creator. But this truth was not handed down in a mystical vision; rather it was self-evident, revealed by rational observation.

The declaration makes no further mention of God, The Founders strove to emphasize that separation from England was an expression of human rights, rather than Divine Right. "The Founders believed that religion could be a healthy force in society—if it were exercised within a zone of personal autonomy," says Kowalski.

There were practical reasons, too. Different Christian sects held majorities in different colonies—some as established churches, with taxpayer support—and religious language that appeared to favor one faith over another might have jeopardized the early union entirely. "In some respects, we bungled into religious liberty," says Charles Haynes, senior scholar at the First Amendment Center and author of several books on religion in public life. "Early on, the religious divisions in the colonies gave us little choice. So, in a way, we have religious diversity to thank for religious liberty."

Religion Left Out of the Constitution

Like the declaration before it, the Constitution is also relatively free of religious-speak. It does not solicit God's blessing; instead, it begins with an invocation of "We, the People." Indeed, the Constitution's only mention of religion is negative—in Article Six, where it expressly commands that "no religious test shall ever be required as a qualification to any office or public trust under the United States."

"The lack of God-language in the Constitution is not an oversight," Kowalski says. "It provoked protest among more orthodox Christians, who thought that government needed some divine sanction." But in the end, a majority voted to keep the Constitution faith-neutral. Meanwhile, some signatories felt that the Constitution did not go far enough to guarantee basic human rights. In response, James Madison proposed a number of amendments; of the ten that comprise the Bill of Rights, the First demarcates our religious freedoms in the plain language of the Establishment Clause which, incidentally, only applies to the federal government. Several states still had established churches, while others prided themselves as havens of conscience. The Establishment Clause split the difference by throwing the issue back to the states. Those with established churches could continue to favor them, while disestablished states were free to remain so.

The true vindication for the Establishment Clause came over the years, as a sense of common American identity began to grow, and states with official churches began, one by one, to disestablish them by acts of legislature.

America Is Religiously Diverse

Since its beginnings, America has been extraordinarily religiously diverse. Although it's true that, as of 1800, the majority of white Americans were Protestants of some kind, that formulation misrepresents the religious landscape of the time and the strained, even hostile relations between various congregations. The American Protestant identity—the tendency of many mainline denominations to downplay their differences and to think of themselves as "Protestant" first and foremost—only developed as immigration and expansion allowed for growth among minority faith groups. The years 1800–1850 saw U.S. population quadruple as Catholics, Lutherans, and Jews arrived from Europe, and as the country acquired territories from France, Spain, and Mexico, making their inhabitants—mostly Catholics—into newly minted U.S. citizens.

Today, as then, the country is experiencing a boom in immigration; and again, immigrants are bringing their faiths with them. Islam is considered to be one of the fastest growing religions in America. According to at least one survey, there are more Buddhists in America now than Evangelical Episcopalians. Some projections indicate that by mid-century, Protestant Americans will be the ones in the minority, a notion that makes many anxious, even now.

Over our country's history, different groups have been singled out as threats to national unity. In the 1800s, Catholics were the bogeyman of choice. Anti-papist preachers warned that we were losing our country to those who did not share American values. Catholics, they claimed, could never be real Americans; they owed their true allegiance to a foreign tyrant and alien laws, and were too superstitious and backward to ever blend into our society.

God in the Pledge

The Pledge of Allegiance is revered today by most Americans. It is recited on a daily basis by millions of public school children and their teachers in classrooms across all fifty states. It concludes every naturalization ceremony. The U.S. Senate opens each legislative session with a collective recital of the Pledge. . . . The Pledge has become the most popular and recognizable of American civil ceremonies. It has also, arguably, accrued religious significance because of its theological referent.

Things were not always so. From its birth in 1892 to 1954, the Pledge of Allegiance made no mention of "God." Baptist minister and Christian Socialist Francis Bellamy had composed the original version for the September 8 issue of *The Youth's Companion*'s quadricentennial commemoration of Christopher Columbus's arrival in the Americas. The Pledge was then modified several times during the National Flag Conferences of 1923 and 1924, until Congress wrote this version into federal law on June 22, 1942: "I pledge allegiance to the Flag of the United States of America and to the Republic for which it stands, one Nation indivisible, with liberty and justice for all." On June 14, 1954, after a successful campaign by the (Catholic) Knights of Columbus and an influential sermon by a Presbyterian minister, Congress added the phrase "under God," and in so doing, embedded belief in God as well as the nation's subordinate relationship to that God within an expression of fidelity to the state.

Grace Y. Kao and Jerome E. Copulsky,
Journal of the American Academy of Religion,
Spring 2007.

If that rhetoric has a familiar ring to it, it's because those same words have been used recently against other immigrant religious groups, particularly Muslims in the wake of the terrorist attacks of September 11, 2001. "Every time we come to a period in our history when we are traumatized, when we are afraid, this anxiety returns us to the idea of recovering the America that's been lost," says Haynes. But Catholics managed to assimilate within a generation or two, and the American Catholic Church proved to be a different sort of institution than the European church, simply because of the cultural and political conditions on the ground. Just so, there's reason to believe that Islam in our democratic, pluralistic society will be unlike Islam practiced elsewhere.

New Denominations Find Freedom

In the 19th century, new denominations founded in the United States would prove vital to the cause of religious freedom— both for their minority status and for doctrines that brought them into conflict with the legal system.

In 1879 the Supreme Court ruled that civil laws trumped the Mormon doctrine of polygamy as a religious duty. Nasty lawsuits and countersuits raged for years, threatening the continued existence of the church itself. In the end, American identity proved so important to the Mormon church that it officially revised its religious doctrine to bring it in line with U.S. law.

But there have been times, too, when the law favored the dictates of religious conscience. In 1943 the Supreme Court reversed a ruling that originally upheld a Pennsylvania school board's expulsion of Jehovah's Witness schoolchildren who refused to salute the flag, but not before the controversy touched off a firestorm in communities across the country, where Witnesses were beaten, run out of town, or even jailed for sedition.

In recent years, the Mormon Church has cast itself as a defender of traditional marriage laws, leading the opposition to marriage rights for gays and lesbians. And by their very unwillingness to engage in secular politics, Jehovah's Witnesses have done the nation a great service in helping strengthen the protection of religious practice from government intrusion.

Maintaining Separation

While the First Amendment keeps government out of religion, it also protects against the flip side: the injection of religion into government, using the political process to pursue essentially moral goals. To be sure, many of our great social movements—abolitionism, temperance, women's rights—had religious foundations, beginning with the idea of inalienable, God-given rights. But in trying to reform American society, some movements misstepped, promoting a particular, and even particularly extreme, religious viewpoint under government auspices. Prohibition, for instance, was enacted in 1920 under pressure from a movement led by Protestant sects. Many of the measure's opponents were also people of faith, who believed that government shouldn't meddle in moral issues.

We'll probably never see Prohibition return; but other battles keep flaring up. In 2004 atheists challenged the recitation of the Pledge of Allegiance in public schools as an unconstitutional endorsement of religion because it contained the words "under God." (The motto "In God We Trust" on U.S. currency has recently come under fire for the same reason.) The Scopes trial of 1925 challenged a Tennessee law banning instruction in evolutionary theory. Eighty years later, the Kansas Board of Education voted to return creationism—calling it "Intelligent Design"—to the classroom. (The vote was reversed in 2007.)

Today, many Americans are confused and angered about the principle of separation, Haynes says. "For people afraid of losing our identity, it only pushes them to be more hostile to the First Amendment. That's dangerous because that principle is the core condition for religious freedom that protects the rights of all."

Proper understanding was just one of the areas addressed at a [2009] conference on the future of religious freedom in America, cosponsored by the First Amendment Center. There, policy experts identified several concerns for the future, including the consensus that free exercise of religion needs more protection still—especially for minority faiths; ways to prevent future backlash against certain religious groups—especially Muslim Americans in the wake of 9/11; and the need to provide more First Amendment education.

"The challenge is to reaffirm our commitment to religious freedom in a way that allows us to address our differences," says Haynes. "It will take a real engagement, as individuals and communities, to find a way to protect the rights of people of all faiths and no faith. I think we can do it, but we can't do it just by hoping for it."

Or praying for it.

| "Americans are slowly becoming less
Christian."

Christianity in America
Is Declining

Barry A. Kosmin and Ariela Keysar

*In 1990, the first American Religious Identification Survey was
conducted to determine the attitudes of Americans in the forty-
eight contiguous states toward religion. A second survey was conducted in 2001, and the results of the third survey, conducted in
2008, are presented in the following viewpoint. Barry A. Kosmin
and Ariela Keysar contend that, in accordance with their data,
the United States is becoming a less Christian nation, as Americans nationwide identify themselves as nontheist or not belonging to any religious group. In comparing the 2008 responses with
those from the earlier surveys, the authors conclude that American self-identification within all Christian groups is similarly declining. Barry A. Kosmin is a sociologist and founding director of
the Institute for the Study of Secularism in Society and Culture
(ISSSC). Ariela Keysar is a demographer and associate director
of the ISSSC. Both are professors at Trinity College in the Public
Policy and Law Program.*

Barry A. Kosmin and Ariela Keysar, *American Religious Identification Survey*, Hartford,
CT: The Institute for the Study of Secularism in Society and Culture, 2009. Copyright ©
ISSSC 2009. Reproduced by permission.

As you read, consider the following questions:

1. According to the authors, by how many million adults has the "Nones" group grown since 1990?

2. As stated by Kosmin and Keysar, what percentage of Americans believe in a "deist or paganistic concept of the Divine as a higher power"?

3. What three religious behaviors do the authors claim have been reduced in significance in contemporary U.S. life?

The U.S. adult population over 18 years of age grew by nearly 53 million persons in the 18 years between 1990 and 2008. As a result, all the religious identification categories ... increased their overall numbers. The most dramatic changes in the balance of religious sentiments seem to have occurred during the 1990s. The changes between 2001 and 2008, when the adult population expanded by over 20 million persons, largely reflect the influence of the heavy immigration primarily from Latin America in recent years.

Fewer Identify as Christian

The 2008 findings confirm the conclusions we came to in our earlier studies that Americans are slowly becoming less Christian and that in recent decades the challenge to Christianity in American society does not come from other world religions or new religious movements (NRMs) but rather from a rejection of all organized religions. To illustrate the point, ... the non-theist and No Religion groups collectively known as "Nones" have gained almost 20 million adults since 1990 and risen from 8.2 to 15.0 percent of the total population. If we include those Americans who either don't know their religious identification (0.9 percent) or refuse to answer our key question (4.1 percent), and who tend to somewhat resemble "Nones" in their social profile and beliefs, we can observe that in 2008 one in five adults does not identify with a religion of any kind compared with one in ten in 1990.

Other non-Christian religious groups and faiths have steadily grown in numbers from a small base and have gained three million adherents since 1990, but they represent only 4 percent of the national population. The various Christian churches and groups gained 31 million adherents to total over 173 million, but their combined numbers as a proportion of the population fell by 10 percent from 86.2 percent down to 76 percent over the past two decades. The nation's largest Christian group, the Catholics, gained 11 million, thanks largely to immigration, and now numbers just over 57 million adult self-identifiers, but the Catholic percentage of the national population still fell from 26.2 percent to 25.1 percent between 1990 and 2008. The Other Christian category, largely composed of adherents of the Protestant Churches and traditions, also gained 11 million people but fell from 60 to 51 percent of the total population. . . .

Growth of the "Nones"

The period 1990–2008 . . . saw the total population grow by 30 percent. As was stated previously every [religious] group has increased in absolute numbers but the rate of growth has varied. The largest net increase in numbers went to the Nones, which have grown by 138% in the period. . . . The Nones also secured nearly 38 percent of the total population increase. Catholics and the Other Christians groups each received around a 21 percent share of the population increase. The Other Religions group rose by 50 percent in absolute numbers and gained 6 percent of the share of the national growth.

The population we know least about, those who do not know or refuse to reveal their religious identification, grew the most rapidly. This reflects social changes in attitudes and in American society over the past two decades. There is less willingness to participate in surveys of all types by the American public. Although this leaves a lacuna [gap] in the ARIS [American Religious Identification Survey] statistics, the overall rate of refusal to participate is low by international standards. For example, the rate of refusal to the religion question in the national U.K. Government 2001 Census was higher at seven percent.

"Plain Christians" Increase

Categorizing and aggregating religious groups is a difficult and controversial task but it is necessary in order to effectively monitor and measure trends. . . . It must be borne in mind that respondents to ARIS could easily and quite legitimately offer a number of terms when answering our key question. The protocol in ARIS is to use the first response offered. In fact over 100 unique response categories were recorded. This is particularly true among the "Other Christian" group where a generic religious tradition response, a theological outlook or belief response or a denominational affiliation response were recorded. In order to try to get some specificity to the answers if an ARIS respondent offers the answer "Christian" or "Protestant" there is then a filter question which asks *What denomination is that?* . . . Over time this further probing has been successful in refining the "Protestant" response category. However, it has not succeeded in curbing the tide of preference for self-identification as a plain "Christian," the numbers of which have doubled since 1990. This trend suggests that among those we categorize as "Other Christian" both personal preferences and collective religious labeling is in flux. . . .

"Baptist" is the majority response category in [the Baptist] tradition, but numerous varieties of Baptist denomination, right down to the level of the local chapel, were offered by respondents. This includes, of course, Southern Baptist and American Baptist. The Baptist population was relatively stable over the 1990s. The sudden growth spurt in Baptist numbers since 2001 seems to reflect a measurable reassertion of a Bap-

Religious Self-identification of the U.S. Adult Population, 1990, 2001, 2008

	1990		2001		2008	
	Estimated Number of People	%	Estimated Number of People	%	Estimated Number of People	%
Catholic	46,004,000	26.2	50,873,000	24.5	57,199,000	25.1
Other Christian	105,221,000	60.0	108,641,000	52.2	116,203,000	50.9
Total Christians	151,225,000	86.2	159,514,000	76.7	173,402,000	76.0
Other Religions	5,853,000	3.3	7,740,000	3.7	8,796,000	3.9
Nones	14,331,000	8.2	29,481,000	14.1	34,169,000	15.0
DK/Refused	4,031,000	2.3	11,246,000	5.4	11,815,000	5.2
Total	**175,440,000**	**100.0**	**207,983,000**	**100.0**	**228,182,000**	**100.0**

TAKEN FROM: American Religious Identification Survey, 2009.

tist identity among the population and more detailed varieties of Baptist were offered by respondents in 2008 than in 2001.

The historic Mainline Christian churches have consistently lost market share since the 1950s, but since 2001 there has been a significant fall in numbers. The Methodists and Episcopalians have been particularly affected by losses. Much of this decline in Mainline identification is due to the growing public preference for the generic "Christian" response and the recent growth in the popularity of the "non-denominational Christian" response. Fewer than 200,000 people favored this term in 1990 but in 2008 it accounts for over eight million Americans. Another notable finding is the rise in the preference to self-identify as "Born Again" or "Evangelical" rather than with any Christian tradition, church or denomination.

The Pentecostal tradition made particular headway during the 1990s but its growth appears to have leveled off recently. The incidence of specific Pentecostal denominational labels such as Assemblies of God or Church of God has varied over the years. The Protestant denominations, mainly composed of conservative and sectarian groups, have grown in size and proportion. The Mormon and Latter Day Saints tradition has slowly but steadily grown throughout this period. The above findings lead us to conclude that among the Christian groups the tendency is to move either to a more sectarian or to a more generalized form of Christian identity at the expense of a denominational identity. These trends also suggest a movement towards more conservative beliefs and particularly to a more "evangelical" outlook among Christians. . . .

Pagan Beliefs Increase

The rise of the Nones has been one of the most important trends on the American religious scene since 1990. The overall rate of growth of those expressing no religious preference slowed after 2001 but the numbers offering a specific self-identification as Agnostic or Atheist rose markedly from over a million in 1990 to about 2 million in 2001 to about 3.6 million today. The historic reluctance of Americans to self-identify in this manner or use these terms seems to have diminished. Nevertheless . . . the level of underreporting of these theological labels is still significant.

A new belief question was introduced into ARIS in 2008. . . . When asked about the existence of God less than 70 percent of Americans now believe in the traditional theological concept of a personal God. This question was not asked in 1990 and 2001. A surprisingly large proportion of contemporary Americans, just over 12 percent, believe in a deist or paganistic concept of the Divine as a higher power. Whereas . . . only one percent of Americans actually self-identify as agnostics, . . . 10 percent hold agnostic beliefs (5.7% a "softer" form and 4.3% a "harder form" of agnosticism). These findings about the "belief" aspect of religiosity tend to complicate our interpretation of some of the trends and findings . . . relating to "belonging." If 76 percent of Americans self-identify with Christianity and 80 percent with a religion then many millions do not subscribe fully to the theology of the groups with which they identify. . . .

Theological Polarization

Respondents [who identified themselves as Christians] were specifically asked *"Do you identify as a Born Again or Evangelical Christian?"* No definition was offered of the terms, which are usually associated with a "personal relationship" with Jesus Christ together with a certain view of salvation, scripture, and missionary work. . . . [Forty-five] percent of all American Christians now self-identify in this manner, and they account for 34 percent of the total national adult population. What is significant is the recent spread of Evangelicalism well beyond Christians affiliated with those groups that are members of the National Evangelical Association so that millions of Mainliners and Catholics now identify with this trend.

There is a real and growing theological polarization in American society whereby 34 percent of the population believe they are "Born Again" but 25–30 percent reject the idea of a personal divinity. These questions on belief reveal the cultural polarization between the pious and non-religious portions of the national population, which are today roughly similar in size.

Religious Ritual Declines

Behavior is the third "B" in the triangle of religiosity, together with belonging and belief. New and unique data, available only in the 2008 survey, ... [reveals] the extent of religious rituals, practices, or sacraments of Americans relating to those life cycle events that have been the traditional preserve of most religions. The proportion of adults who have undergone a religious initiation of some kind is reduced somewhat by the large number of Baptists in the American population who delay baptism into the adult years. However, for most people this was a decision made by their parents so the statistics (given the median age of the adult population) really reflect religious practice in an earlier generation, that is to say, on average, around 1960.

The religious marriage question relates to a more recent and personal decision by the actual respondents but it is probably also a negotiated decision with the spouse. Nevertheless there is a significant minority, 30 percent of married couples, that has rejected a religious marriage ceremony. It is the final question that relates to expectation of a religious funeral which is probably the most revealing of social trends today. Funerals and interments are important if one has personal concerns about salvation and the immortality of the soul. It appears that over one-fourth of contemporary Americans are unconcerned with such religious ideas. Overall the trend ... though not definitive does suggest a slight erosion of participation in religious rituals over their own life cycles by our 2008 respondents.

The findings and patterns ... related to current patterns of religious belonging, belief and behavior seem to show a high degree of correlation. They reveal that the United States in 2008 can be characterized as a country with a Christian majority population but with a growing non-religious or irreligious minority. The growing non-religious minority reduces the traditional societal role of congregations and places of worship in family celebrations of life-cycle events. Forestalling of religious rites of passage, such as marriage, and the lowering expectations on religious funeral services, could have long-lasting consequences for religious institutions.

"*Reports of Christianity's demise in America have been greatly exaggerated.*"

The Decline of Christianity in America Has Been Exaggerated

Ed Stetzer

While many studies have shown a decline in the number of Americans who identify themselves as Christians, many experts insist that these statistics in no way suggest that the religion is on the verge of becoming obsolete in U.S. society. In the viewpoint that follows, Ed Stetzer argues that much of the research showing the decreasing proportion of self-identified Christians has been exaggerated and used to incorrectly show that the country is becoming irreligious. While troubled by the loss of followers from certain Christian denominations, Stetzer maintains that the increases within other denominations, such as evangelical Christianity, is a cause for reassurance that Americans remain committed to Christian values. Ed Stetzer is coauthor of the book Lost and Found: The Younger Unchurched and the

Ed Stetzer, "Chicken Little Was Wrong," *Christianity Today*, vol. 54, January 2010, pp. 34–37. Reproduced by permission of the author.

Churches That Reach Them *and the president of LifeWay, a company that produces Christian publications, music, educational programs, and other products.*

As you read, consider the following questions:

1. As stated by Stetzer, what is the attraction of bad statistics and what are the negative effects of believing in them?

2. According to the author, what myth did the Baylor Religion Survey expose?

3. What concerns Stetzer more than the data showing the number of adherents to a particular Christian faith?

The reporter's question was one of the best I had ever been asked. "Why do you evangelicals love to make up and say such bad things about yourselves?"

Great question, I thought. But I'm here to talk about social science research, not abnormal psychology.

I was facing a room full of reporters in a Religion Newswriters Association session at the *Washington Post* building in [Washington,] D.C. They had invited me to explain the difference between good religious research and bad. It's a real problem. News reports are always batting around some new bit of bad research. And sometimes a snippet from good research gets pulled out of context, then mangled, garbled, and spewed all over.

The Importance of Terminology

Once a choice morsel of misinformation gets out, it multiplies faster than dandelions in the spring. We have all heard these soul-seizing yet false factoids. Some of us have even repeated them:

"Christianity will die out in this generation unless we do something now."

"Only 4 percent of this generation is Christian."

"Ninety-four percent of teenagers drop out of church, never to return again."

And perhaps my favorite: "With its 195 million un-churched people [those who do not attend religious services regularly], America has become the new mission field. America has more unchurched people than the entire populations of all but 11 of the world's 194 nations." The "195 million un-churched people" statistic is all over the place—from books to blogs to church bulletins. And those who quote it often at-tribute it to researcher George Barna.

The problem is, it isn't true. That's not what the research showed, and Barna wasn't the one who conducted the study.

The original stat came out of a project I was a part of while working with the Southern Baptist Convention's North American Mission Board (NAMB). We researched the number of unbelievers in the U.S., not the number of unchurched people. But someone somewhere changed the language, and thus the meaning.

Impact of Bad Statistics

Three years ago [in 2007], *Christianity Today* sister magazine *Books & Culture* carried a provocative article by Christian Smith entitled, "Evangelicals Behaving Badly with Statistics." Smith, a highly respected professor of sociology at the Univer-sity of Notre Dame, declared that American evangelicals "are among the worst abusers of simple descriptive statistics."

He went on to dissect an advertisement for a summit that declared, "Christianity in America won't survive another de-cade unless we do something now." The summit organizers claimed that only 4 percent of today's teenagers would be evangelical believers by the time they became adults. "We are on the verge of a catastrophe!" the advertisement screamed.

As it turns out, that 4 percent statistic comes from an in-formal survey of 211 young people in three states conducted by a seminary professor nine years earlier. Smith affirmed the

professor's approach but explained that an unwarranted infer-
ence was drawn from a small, non-representative sample to
reach conclusions about the future faith conditions of entire
generations.

Smith wrote, "Why do evangelicals recurrently abuse statistics? My observation is that they are usually trying desper-
ately to attract attention and raise people's concern in order to
mobilize resources and action for some cause. . . . Evangelical
leaders and organizations routinely use descriptive statistics in
sloppy, unwarranted, misrepresenting, and sometimes absolutely preposterous ways, usually to get attention and sound
alarms, at least some of which are false alarms."

My friends at NAMB and my boss, Thom Rainer (the
originator of the 4 percent statistic), accurately reported their
methods and conclusions. But the research took on a life of its
own. Unfortunately, good people who are trying to help the
church change its bad habits in order to reach a lost world often misappropriate the research. Evangelical Christianity in
the U.S. undoubtedly faces serious challenges, but hyperventi-
lating doesn't help—even when the statistics are accurate. Cry-
ing, "The sky is falling!" might sell books, but it never fixes
problems.

I suspect that we are attracted to bad statistics mostly for
motivation. We need a personal push and hope to give one to
our churches as well. But bad stats can feed self-loathing and
lethargy as much as they can encourage steadfastness in mission.

Evangelical Christianity on the Rise

Another way we misrepresent the state of American Christianity is by seizing upon one startling aspect of a study and pulling it out of context, sometimes ignoring other findings in the
study. This happened with the American Religious Identification Survey (ARIS), released in March 2009. It found a significant decline in religion and a rise in secularism that set news
outlets buzzing.

"The percentage of Americans who call themselves Christians has dropped dramatically over the past two decades, and those who do are increasingly identifying themselves without traditional denomination labels," wrote Michelle Boorstein of the *Washington Post*. Cathy Lynn Grossman at *USA Today* reported, "The percentage of people who call themselves in some way Christian has dropped more than 11 percent in a generation. The faithful have scattered out of their traditional bases: The Bible Belt is less Baptist. The Rust Belt is less Catholic. And everywhere, more people are exploring spiritual frontiers or falling off the faith map completely."

The ARIS correctly observed that denominations and denominationalism are in decline, the cultural influence of Christianity continues to slip, more people are describing themselves as nonreligious (now 15 percent), and minority religions like Islam and Wicca are becoming more popular.

Some observers also latched onto the ARIS finding that nonreligious Americans have dramatically increased in number, and concluded that evangelical Christianity in the U.S. is on the verge of annihilation. But the ARIS finding was only half the equation.

The ARIS also reveals a simultaneous increase in the number of Americans who self-identify as evangelical Christians. There is a lot in the ARIS that should be disturbing to the church, but the decline in the percentage of self-identified Christians that the ARIS found falls far short of a great crackup in evangelicalism.

Complete Analysis Necessary

One of the first things you learn in research is that there are many ways to look at things. Every time we have new data from a well-designed study, it helps us. But one conclusion from one study is no foundation for a theory on the future of a society.

To get the whole picture, responsible researchers look at various studies, their methodologies, and their results. We must understand the parts in light of the whole. We should interpret each finding in light of the full study, and interpret each study in light of other studies. We reach bad conclusions when we latch onto one finding of one study, drag it out of context, and proclaim it from the rooftops without knowing whether our interpretation is justified.

The ARIS: Perhaps its most interesting finding was the stunning decline of Catholicism in the Northeast.

In addition to that trend, 15 percent of Americans claimed no religion at all. The growth that did occur in the Christian population was among those who would identify only as "Christian," "evangelical/born again," or "nondenominational Christian." These groups, 5 percent of the population in 1990, stood at 11.8 percent in 2008.

General Social Survey (GSS): One relevant aspect of the GSS (conducted every other year since 1972) is the snapshot it provides about worship service attendance. My book *Lost and Found* included a 1972–2006 GSS chart that showed that the percentage of 20-somethings attending weekly worship services has been rising since 2000, after a serious dip in the mid-1990s. My co-authors and I admitted that only time would tell if the rising trajectory would continue. Since then, the 2008 data showed another uptick, bringing attendance among evangelical 20-somethings back to what it was in 1972. Among non-evangelicals there was indeed a decline: Just fewer than 25 percent attended weekly in 1972. In 2008, it was just over 12 percent. Listening to some commentators, you might conclude that young adults had left the church. But that is not what the data tell us.

Gallup: In April 2009, Gallup reported that church attendance among Protestant young adults rebounded in the 1980s and is now close to the level it was in the 1950s. Of course, "Protestant" covers a wide range of denominations, some of which have experienced high membership growth, others of which have declined. Gallup generally hasn't shown any change in reported church attendance, much less a massive decline among 20-somethings.

To be fair, these numbers are likely influenced by the "halo effect," where people are more likely to say they go to church than to actually go. People always inflate reports of behaviors when they perceive that the behavior in question is desirable. It's significant, though, that the numbers on weekly church attendance haven't changed substantially. If Christianity were in steep decline, the social desirability of it would be, too—which would reduce the halo effect.

Baylor Religion Survey: The 2007 Baylor Religion Survey, reported in [American sociologist of religion] Rodney Stark's book *What Americans Really Believe* (2008), found that, of the 11 percent of Americans who said they had "no religion," two-thirds expressed some belief in God. In addition, many were not "irreligious" but merely "unchurched." More to the point, the study found that people do not use activities of the "scattered" church—religious activities not affiliated with or sponsored by a congregation—as a substitute for participation in the "gathered" church.

The study exposed as a myth a widespread dissatisfaction with organized religion. Of those who are engaged in "scattered" activities, such as prayer and Bible study groups, 80 percent frequently attend church. While many Americans are disillusioned with organized religion, theirs is by no means the prevailing attitude. Organized churches face serious issues, but the facts simply do not support the mantra that churches are dying out.

Pew Forum on Religion and Public Life: A 2008 study conducted by the Pew Forum found that 40 percent of religiously unaffiliated people say religion is still important in their lives. Further, the research found that the "unaffiliated" group does a lousy job of retaining adherents. Pew found that

39 percent of those who grew up unaffiliated are now Protestant, most of them evangelical, while another 15 percent now affiliate with Catholicism or another faith. Though we hear a great deal about young people leaving the church, we hear few reports about the stream of young people coming into the church.

Hard to Generalize

It's hard to generalize about American Christianity. The scene is just too diverse. But the most reputable studies give us certain indicators about particular denominations and the spiritual lives of U.S. adults. Mainline denominations are no longer bleeding; they are hemorrhaging. Increasingly, they are simply managing their decline. For evangelicals, the picture is better, but only in comparison to the mainline churches. Southern Baptists, composing the largest Protestant denomination in the U.S., have apparently peaked and are trending toward decline. The same is true of most evangelical denominations. Only 2 of the top 25 Christian denominations are growing: the Assemblies of God and the Church of God (Cleveland, Tennessee). Both are Pentecostal.

Still, those worried about church decline are worried about data beyond the simple "more" or "less" numbers. The bigger concern is that people who identify themselves as Christians (and even evangelicals) do not evidence the beliefs historically held by Christians.

The Shape of Faith to Come, a 2008 book by [vice president of the Christian publishing company B&H Publishing Group] Brad Waggoner (and based on a [Christian product and service provider] LifeWay Research study), evaluated seven domains of spiritual formation: learning truth, obeying God and denying self, serving God and others, sharing Christ, exercising faith, seeking God, and building relationships. It found that only 17 percent of Protestant churchgoers in America scored the equivalent of 80 percent or higher in those key ar-

---

Faith Is an Intrinsic Human Impulse

Religious doubt and diversity have . . . always been quint-essentially American. [French political philosopher and historian] Alexis de Tocqueville said that "the religious atmosphere of the country was the first thing that struck me on arrival in the United States," but he also discovered a "great depth of doubt and indifference" to faith. [Thomas] Jefferson had earlier captured the essence of the American spirit about religion when he observed that his statute for religious freedom in Virginia was "meant to comprehend, within the mantle of its protection, the Jew and the Gentile, the Christian and the Mahometan [Muslim], the Hindoo and infidel of every denomination"—and those of no faith whatever. The American culture of religious liberty helped create a busy free market of faith: by disestablishing churches, the nation made religion more popular, not less.

America, then, is not a post-religious society—and cannot be as long as there are people in it, for faith is an intrinsic human impulse. The belief in an order or a reality beyond time and space is ancient and enduring. "All men," said [ancient Greek poet] Homer, "need the gods."

Jon Meacham,
Newsweek, April 13, 2009.

---

eas of Christian discipleship. A full 57 percent of respondents said they had not once explained to another person in the past six months how to become a Christian. Then, over the course of the next year, only 3.5 percent showed a net increase in spiritual growth. These data are cause for concern, for sure. The church cannot grow if Christians are not actively discipling new believers.

Changing, Not Dying

Reports of Christianity's demise in America have been greatly exaggerated. While the main thrust of good research does indicate that the percentage of Americans who self-identify as Christians is declining, these data are not necessarily a bad thing. If three out of four Americans call themselves Christians, we are in big trouble. Three out of four Americans certainly do not live like Christians. Christianity becomes confused when everyone is a Christian but no one is following Christ. We evangelicals believe that most Americans do not have a relationship with Jesus Christ.

There is little doubt in my mind that the cultural expression of Christianity in America is declining. True, Christianity is losing its "home-field advantage" in North America. At the same time, some trends tell us we are seeing the growth of a more robust Christian faith and commitment. We are seeing some abandon nominal Christianity, and many others retain an authentic Christian faith. Christianity in North America is not going to die out in this generation or any other, even though it is going through an identity crisis of sorts.

In the meantime, bad and misinterpreted data must not convince us that organized Christianity in America is dead and gone. Facts are our friends. The facts tell us that the church in North America is struggling but also, in many places, growing. Discerning research can help us diagnose our condition. It may even help the church find strategic means to address the mission field right outside our doors. And ultimately, we all can agree that a declining church needs the unchanging gospel.

Periodical Bibliography

The following articles have been selected to supplement the diverse views presented in this chapter.

Tom Bethell — "Our Permanent Revolution," *American Spectator*, March 2007.

Charles M. Blow — "Paranormal Flexibility," *New York Times*, December 12, 2009.

Christianity Today — "Mega-mirror," August 2009.

Douglas Farrow — "The Audacity of the State," *Touchstone: A Journal of Mere Christianity*, January 2010.

Tom Flynn — "Secularization Renewed?" *Free Inquiry*, June/July 2009.

James F. Harris — "Religion and Liberal Democracy," *Humanist*, May/June 2006.

Kevin J. "Seamus" Hasson — "The Myth," *American Spectator*, February 2008.

Josef Joffe — "The God Gap," *American Interest*, November/December 2009.

Barry W. Lynn — "Persistently Wrong: The Religious Right Must Accept Its Losses," *Church & State*, January 2010.

Daniel McCarthy — "Every Man a God-King," *American Conservative*, October 1, 2009.

Jeff Sharlet — "Jesus Killed Mohammed," *Harper's*, May 2009.

John Tomasin — "Clear Proof America Is Not a 'Christian Nation,'" *Free Inquiry*, February/March 2008.

OPPOSING VIEWPOINTS® SERIES

CHAPTER 2

What Effect Does Religion Have on American Society?

Chapter Preface

Religion and politics have enjoyed a fair amount of separation in the United States since the nation's founding, in large part due to clauses in the Constitution, especially in the Bill of Rights, which ensures that "Congress shall make no law respecting an establishment of religion" nor prohibit "the free exercise thereof." While the country's founding documents suggest this separation, nearly every president has included a measure of religious language in his speech making. References to a divine creator have often served as an opportunity for a politician to unite Americans behind a common cause. Following the 2000 presidential elections, however, religion became a tool for politicians to rally groups of voters behind their individual candidacies. Nationwide, candidates began focusing their campaigns around religious concerns, and voters began to consider the religious convictions and affiliations of candidates more seriously as they entered the voting booth, thus forging a new bond between politics and religion in the United States.

The 2000 George W. Bush presidential campaign was one of the main catalysts in establishing the new link. Throughout the Republican primary and presidential race, the campaign openly courted conservative, evangelical Christian voters, emphasizing the candidate's beliefs as a born-again Christian as well as his strict adherence to Republican values. With Bush's victory, it became clear that a religiously centered campaign had a remarkable ability to reach voters. The focus on religion recommenced during the 2004 presidential campaign, throughout which liberal commentators vocally lamented the erosion of the separation of church and state in politics and its consequences for the country. Communications professor David Domke critiqued Bush's tactics and policy making, calling them "a modern form of political fundamentalism—that is, the adaptation of a self-proclaimed conservative Christian rectitude, by way of strategic language choice and communication approaches designed for a mass-media culture, into political policy."

While at once criticizing Bush's infusion of religion into politics, liberals were at the same time formulating strategies to inject religion into their own campaigns to counter what they saw as the growing connection between Republicans and the one-in-five voters who reported in the 2004 exit polls that "moral values" were the deciding factor in choosing a president. During the democratic primary and the presidential campaign of 2008, candidates struggled to define themselves as committed believers, each proclaiming the significance faith played in their personal lives and their work as politicians. The expert on evangelicals at the Ethics and Public Policy Center, Michael Cromartie, noted, "This really is a big shift in American politics for Democratic candidates to not be shy about their faith and the implications for how they vote."

While the Democratic candidate, Barack Obama, was successful in the 2008 elections, it is difficult to determine whether the focus on religion made the difference as the country faced the largest economic downturn in decades and a rising unemployment rate. Further downplaying the importance of religion, a Pew Forum on Religion & Public Life study reported in 2008 that an increasing number of Americans believe religion should be left out of politics. The appropriate relationship between politics and religion presents only one point of debate in the larger discussion over the role of religion in U.S. society. The authors of the viewpoints in the following chapter examine the beneficial and detrimental effects of religion in both the public and private lives of Americans.

| "*Considerable research has emerged that demonstrates the benefits of religious practice within society.*"

Religion Benefits American Society

Patrick F. Fagan

The correlation between religious beliefs and positive social outcomes has long been the subject of sociological study. In the viewpoint that follows, Patrick F. Fagan contends that the body of research examining the impact of religion on society has conclusively shown that religious practice can be connected with numerous benefits such as improved marriages, better family relations, an interest in education, and well-connected communities. Fagan presents a comprehensive analysis of studies conducted on the social impacts of religion since the 1950s to support his claim that religion is one of the best tools that can be used to address many of the problems faced by U.S. society today. Patrick F. Fagan is a senior fellow and the director of the Center for Research on Marriage and Religion, a division of the Family Research Council, a conservative, Christian public policy organization.

Patrick F. Fagan, "Why Religion Matters Even More: The Impact of Religious Practice on Social Stability," *Heritage Foundation Backgrounder #1992*, December 18, 2006. Copyright © 2006 The Heritage Foundation. Reproduced by permission.

As you read, consider the following questions:

1. As stated by the author, spouses who rate their religious beliefs as "very important" are how much less likely to get a divorce than those who only rate their religious beliefs as "somewhat important"?

2. According to Fagan, how does the religious practice of parents influence their children's education?

3. What positive behaviors does Fagan claim religion instills in youth at risk of using drugs and committing crimes in impoverished neighborhoods?

Over the past decade, considerable research has emerged that demonstrates the benefits of religious practice within society. Religious practice promotes the well-being of individuals, families, and the community.

Of particular note are the studies that indicate the benefits of religion to the poor. Regular attendance at religious services is linked to healthy, stable family life, strong marriages, and well-behaved children. The practice of religion also leads to a reduction in the incidence of domestic abuse, crime, substance abuse, and addiction. In addition, religious practice leads to an increase in physical and mental health, longevity, and education attainment. Moreover, these effects are intergenerational, as grandparents and parents pass on the benefits to the next generations. . . .

Religious Belief Aids Marriages

There are many indications that the combination of religious practice and stable marital relationships contributes to a strong and successful next generation. We already know that stable marriage is associated with improved physical, intellectual, mental, and emotional health of men, women, and children, as well as equipping them with the values and habits that promote prosperous economic activity. Religious practice is also related to positive outcomes for the stability and quality of marriage.

Numerous sociological studies have shown that valuing religion and regularly practicing it are associated with greater marital stability, higher levels of marital satisfaction, and an increased likelihood that an individual will be inclined to marry. [Sociologist] Christopher Ellison of the University of Texas at Austin and his colleagues found that couples who acknowledged a divine purpose in their marriage were more likely to collaborate, to have greater marital adjustment, and to perceive more benefits from marriage and were less likely to use aggression or to come to a stalemate in their disagreements. Earlier research found that couples whose marriages lasted 30 years or more reported that their faith helped them to deal with difficult times, was a source of moral guidance in making decisions and dealing with conflict, and encouraged them to maintain their commitment to their marriages.

Four of every 10 children experience parental divorce, but a link between religious practice and a decreased likelihood of divorce has been established in numerous studies. Women who are more religious are less likely to experience divorce or separation than their less religious peers. Marriages in which both spouses attend religious services frequently are 2.4 times less likely to end in divorce than marriages in which neither spouse worships. Those who view their religious beliefs as "very important" are 22 percent less likely to divorce than those for whom religious beliefs are only "somewhat important." The sociological literature reviews by the late [psychiatrist] David Larson of the Duke University Medical School and his colleagues indicated that religious attendance is the most important predictor of marital stability, confirming studies conducted as far back as 50 years ago. . . .

Religion Strengthens Families

In general, religious participation appears to foster an authoritative, warm, active, and expressive style of parenting. In addition, parents who attend religious services are more likely to enjoy a better relationship with their children and are more likely to be involved with their children's education. Moreover, the greater a child's religious involvement, the more likely both the child and parent will agree about the quality of their relationship, the more similar their values will be, and the greater their emotional closeness will be. However, some of the same research also shows that religious differences within families can detract from the parent-child relationship.

Compared with mothers who did not consider religion important, those who deemed religion to be very important rated their relationship with their child significantly higher, according to a 1999 study. When mothers and their children share the same level of religious practice, they experience better relationships with one another. For instance, when 18-year-olds attended religious services with approximately the same frequency as their mothers, the mothers reported significantly better relationships with them, even many years later, indicating that the effects of similar religious practice endures. Moreover, mothers who became more religious throughout the first 18 years of their child's life reported a better relationship with that child, regardless of the level of their religious practice before the child was born. Mothers who attended religious services less often over time reported a lower-quality relationship with their adult child.

Grandmothers' religious practice illustrates an intergenerational influence. The more religious a mother's mother is, the more likely the mother has a good relationship with her own child.

Greater religious practice of fathers is associated with better relationships with their children, higher expectations for good relationships in the future, a greater investment in their relationships with their children, a greater sense of obligation to stay in regular contact with their children, and a greater likelihood of supporting their children and grandchildren.

[Sociologist W. Bradford] Wilcox found that fathers' religious affiliations and religious attendance were positively associated with their involvement in activities with their children, such as one-on-one interaction, having dinner with their families, and volunteering for youth-related activities. Compared with fathers who had no religious affiliation, those who attended religious services frequently were more likely to monitor their children, praise and hug their children, and spend time with their children. In fact, fathers' frequency of religious attendance was a stronger predictor of paternal involvement in one-on-one activities with children than were employment and income—the factors most frequently cited in the academic literature on fatherhood. . . .

Devotion Decreases Non-marital Sex

Religious practice and placing a high significance on religion are associated with decreased non-marital sexual activity. After parental marriage, religious practice is probably the most significant factor related to reduced teen sexual activity. Analysis of data from the National Longitudinal Survey of Adolescent Health found that a one-unit increase in religiosity reduced the odds of becoming sexually active by 16 percent for girls and by 12 percent for boys. Another study found that traditional values and religious beliefs were among the most common factors cited by teens as their reason for remaining sexually abstinent, second only to fear (e.g., fear of an unwanted pregnancy, a sexually transmitted disease, or parental discipline). The level of overall religious practice in a community also influences the sexual behavior of its youth: The greater the level of religious practice, the lower the level of teen sexual activity.

In a 2002 review of the academic literature on the effects of religion, 97 percent of the studies reported significant correlations between increased religious involvement and a lower likelihood of promiscuous sexual behaviors. The authors found that individuals with higher levels of religious commitment and those who regularly attended religious services were generally much less likely to engage in premarital sex or extramarital affairs or to have multiple sexual partners.

Thirty-seven percent of births now occur out of wedlock, with an increasing number born to cohabiting parents. However, given the findings on the relationship between religious practice and non-marital sex, attitudes, and behavior, it is not surprising that regular religious practice is one of the most powerful factors in preventing out-of-wedlock births. Rates of such births are markedly higher among young women who do not have a religious affiliation than among peers who do.

The level of young women's religious commitment also makes a significant difference. Compared with those who viewed themselves as being "very religious," those who were "not at all religious" were far more likely to bear a child out of wedlock (among whites, three times as likely; among Hispanics, 2.5 times as likely; and among blacks, twice as likely). At the state aggregate level, the same phenomenon occurs. States with higher rates of religious attendance have lower rates of teenage pregnancy.

Religious Practice Limits Substance Abuse

Numerous studies demonstrate a significant association between religious practice and healthy behavioral habits relating to cigarettes, alcohol, and drugs. Individuals with higher levels of religious involvement have lower rates of abuse and addiction and are more likely to find long-lasting success if they ever struggled with any of these behaviors.

[Psychiatrist] Harold Koenig and colleagues at Duke University found that religious activity was inversely related to cigarette consumption among the elderly. The late [demographer and sociologist] Feroz Ahmed and colleagues at Howard University found the same for African-American women of childbearing age.

Decades of research indicate that a higher level of religious involvement is associated with a reduced likelihood of abusing alcohol or drugs. The relationship between religious practice and the avoidance or moderate use of alcohol is well documented, whether or not denominational tenets specifically prohibit the use of alcohol.

Adolescents, psychiatric patients, and recovering addicts all show lower rates of alcohol abuse the more frequently they engage in religious activities. For adolescents, higher levels of religious practice by their mothers are related to significantly lower rates of alcohol abuse, even after controlling for religious denomination and the adolescents' peer associations—two factors that also influence the level of drinking.

Just as with alcohol, religious practice has for some time predicted significant reduction of substance abuse. In a comprehensive review of the academic literature on religion and substance abuse, [social sciences professor] Byron Johnson of Baylor University and his colleagues reported that, in the vast majority of studies, participation in religious activities was associated with less drug abuse. Even in cases in which individuals used drugs, the more religious were less likely to develop long-term problems. All of the factors related to a decrease in drug use—good family relations, doing well in school, having friends who do not use drugs, and having anti-drug attitudes—had an even more powerful deterrent effect when teenagers were also religious. The more dangerous the drug, the more religious practice deterred its use.

Just as religious practice and belief deter drug abuse, religion also has a positive effect in the treatment of drug addiction. In 1994, a seven-year follow-up study of Teen Challenge, a faith-based drug addiction program, found that the program's graduates had significantly changed their behavior, in contrast to those who had dropped out. A Northwestern University study also found that Teen Challenge participants were more likely to remain sober and to maintain employment than were peers in control groups. . . .

Religion Promotes Education

Because education is important for all citizens, and the government invests heavily in public schooling, any factor that promotes academic achievement is important to the common good. Academic expectations, level of education attained, school attendance, and academic performance are all positively affected by religious practice. In two literature reviews conducted by [sociology professor] Mark Regnerus of the University of Texas at Austin, educational attainment aspirations and math and reading scores correlated positively with more frequent religious practice.

Parents' religious practice also counts. The greater the parents' religious involvement, the more likely they will have higher educational expectations of their children and will communicate with their children regarding schooling. Their children will be more likely to pursue advanced courses, spend more time on homework, establish friendships with academically oriented peers, avoid cutting classes, and successfully complete their degrees.

Students in religiously affiliated schools tend to exhibit a higher level of academic achievement than their peers in secular schools, particularly in low-income urban neighborhoods. For example, studies continue to find that inner-city students in public schools lag behind in educational achievement, compared with students in Catholic schools.

The cultural values of a religious community are also a significant pathway to academic success for adolescents. For example, to earn a high school diploma or take advanced math courses, children must plan for the future and structure their activities accordingly. Religious communities typically invest in forming an ethic of such discipline and persistence. A recent study confirms both this indirect contribution of reli-

Christians and Climate Change

There is hopeful news about climate change. A church revival is happening. The church is expanding its understanding of community to one that is large enough to allow plants and animals to be seen as beloved parts of the heart and household of God. Christians recognize something flawed in a concept that justifies driving species to extinction for the sake of profit or because of the worries of this life and the deceitfulness of riches. This renaissance shares a greater sense of interconnectedness with nature and recognizes the link between our environmental impact and our moral responsibility. I am not responsible for all contributors to climate change. I am responsible, however, for the car I drive, the light bulbs I buy, the ecosystems I protect, and the conservation laws I support.

Peter Illyn,
Creation Care, Fall 2008.

gious community values and the direct influence of the students' own religious activities in promoting academic achievement.

Earlier studies found this same relationship between religious practice and academic discipline. For example, in 1985, the groundbreaking work of [economist] Richard Freeman of Harvard University revealed that attendance at religious services and activities positively affected inner-city youth school attendance, work activity, and allocation of time—all of which were further linked to a decreased likelihood of engaging in deviant activities. For instance, youth who frequently attended religious services were five times less likely to skip school, compared with peers who seldom or never attended. . . .

Religion Benefits Communities

Religious practice benefits not only individuals, but also communities. Religiously active men and women are often more sensitive to others, more likely to serve and give to those in need, and more likely to be productive members of their communities.

Religious practice is linked to greater generosity in charitable giving. In extensive research documenting the relationship between religion and philanthropy, [economist and public policy analyst] Arthur Brooks of Syracuse University demonstrated that religious practice correlates with a higher rate of care and concern for others. Compared with peers with no religious affiliation, religious respondents were 15 percent more likely to report having tender, concerned feelings for the disadvantaged. This gap was reduced by only 2 percent when the effects of education, income, marital status, sex, race, and age were taken into account. . . .

Just as the stable marriage of parents is powerful in preventing crime, so too is the practice of religion. A review of the literature on religion and crime suggests that, compared with less religious counterparts, religiously involved individuals are less likely to carry or use weapons, fight, or exhibit violent behavior. At the metropolitan level of analysis, areas with high rates of congregational membership and areas with high levels of religious homogeneity tend to have lower homicide and suicide rates than other metropolitan areas. Similarly, at the state level of analysis, states with more religious populations tend to have fewer homicides and fewer suicides. . . .

Even against the odds, in neighborhoods of disorder and poverty, religious practice serves as a significant buffer against drug abuse and juvenile delinquency. A study of 2,358 young black males from impoverished inner-city Chicago and Philadelphia found that a high level of religious attendance was associated with a 46 percent reduction in the likelihood of using drugs, a 57 percent reduction in the probability of dealing drugs, and a 39 percent decrease in the likelihood of committing a crime that was not drug-related. Thus, religious attendance was associated with direct decreases in both minor and major forms of crime and deviance to an extent unrivalled by government welfare programs.

The effect of religion is not solely a matter of external controls that curb adolescents' risky behavior. Rather, religious attendance also promotes self-control, a positive allocation of time, attendance at school, and engagement in work. In addition, youth religious practice is linked to a decreased likelihood of associating with delinquent peers—a significant factor in youth crime. . . .

Religious Practice Can Improve Society

A steadily increasing body of evidence from the social sciences demonstrates that regular religious practice benefits individuals, families, and communities, and thus the nation as a whole. The practice of religion improves health, academic achievement, and economic well-being and fosters self-control, self-esteem, empathy, and compassion.

Religious belief and practice can address many of the nation's most pressing social problems, some of which have reached serious levels (e.g., out-of-wedlock births and family dissolution). Research has linked the practice of religion to reductions in the incidence of divorce, crime, delinquency, drug and alcohol addiction, out-of-wedlock births, health problems, anxiety, and prejudice. Faith-based outreach has been uniquely effective in drug addiction rehabilitation and societal re-entry programs for prisoners. Furthermore, the effects of religious belief and practice are intergenerational and cumulative. In a sense, they "compound the interest" of our social capital.

Allan Bergin, a research psychologist who received the American Psychological Association's top award in 1990, summed up the impact of religion in his acceptance address:

"Some religious influences have a modest impact whereas another portion seems like the mental equivalent of nuclear energy."

Freedom from an established religion is compatible with the freedom to fully practice one's religious beliefs. This freedom is very different from purported protection *from* religious influence. To work to reduce the influence of religious belief or practice is to further the disintegration of society. Some may be uncomfortable with the religious beliefs and practices of others, but that discomfort is small compared to the effects of having a society with little or no religious practice. America's ongoing national experiment with freedom now faces anew the challenge of balancing society's need for the benefits that religion brings, its commitment to religious pluralism in the political order, and the rights of those who choose to live with no religious conviction.

Our Founding Fathers, in their dedication to liberty, promoted the freedom of all Americans to practice religious beliefs, or not, as they choose. Although the freedom not to practice religion is intrinsic to religious freedom, that protection does not mean that this non-practice of religion is equally beneficial to society. Social science data reinforce George Washington's declaration in his farewell address: "Of all the dispositions and habits which lead to political prosperity, Religion and Morality are indispensable supports."

"*The most theistic prosperous democracy, the U.S., ... is almost always the most dysfunctional of the developed democracies.*"

Religion Has Not Benefited American Society

Gregory S. Paul

While the United States is considered by some to be exceptional in its retention of Christianity and its rejection of a move toward a more secular society (in accordance with European trends), Gregory S. Paul argues in the following viewpoint that American exceptionality in this sense may not be positive. After surveying a wide range of data analyzing the social health of "prosperous democracies" in western Europe and Japan, Paul comes to the conclusion that the United States is generally more dysfunctional by comparison. As a result, Paul contends that religiosity has not led to improved social conditions for the United States. Gregory S. Paul is a researcher and author who, after initially working in the paleontology field, shifted his focus to what he has termed the "moral-creator socioeconomic hypothesis."

Gregory S. Paul, "Cross-National Correlations of Quantifiable Societal Health with Popular Religiosity and Secularism in the Prosperous Democracies: A First Look," *Journal of Religion and Society*, vol. 7, 2005. Copyright © 2005 Journal of Religion and Society. www.creighton.edu/jrs. Reproduced by permission.

As you read, consider the following questions:

1. As stated by the author, upon what view of the United States do many Americans agree?

2. According to Paul, how do homicide and STD rates in the theistic United States compare with rates in secular Europe?

3. What societal conditions characteristic of "cultures of life" does Paul believe secular, pro-evolution democracies have come the closest to achieving?

Two centuries ago there was relatively little dispute over the existence of God, or the societally beneficial effect of popular belief in a creator. In the twentieth century extensive secularization occurred in western nations, the United States being the only significant exception. If religion has receded in some western nations, what is the impact of this unprecedented transformation upon their populations? Theists often assert that popular belief in a creator is instrumental towards providing the moral, ethical and other foundations necessary for a healthy, cohesive society. Many also contend that widespread acceptance of evolution, and/or denial of a creator, is contrary to these goals. But a cross-national study verifying these claims has yet to be published. That radically differing worldviews can have measurable impact upon societal conditions is plausible according to a number of mainstream researchers. Agreement with the hypothesis that belief in a creator is beneficial to societies is largely based on assumption, anecdotal accounts, and on studies of limited scope and quality restricted to one population. . . .

Societal Health and Religiosity

In the United States many conservative theists consider evolutionary science a leading contributor to social dysfunction because it is amoral or worse, and because it inspires disbelief in a moral creator. The original full title for the creationist Discovery Institute was the Discovery Institute for the Renewal of Science and Culture (a title still applied to a division), and the institute's mission challenges "materialism on specifically scientific grounds" with the intent of reversing "some of materialism's destructive cultural consequences." The strategy for achieving these goals is the "wedge" strategy to insert intelligent design creationism into mainstream academe and subsequently destroy Darwinian science. . . . Politically and socially powerful conservatives have deliberately worked to elevate popular concerns over a field of scientific and industrial research to such a level that it qualifies as a major societal fear factor. The current [2005] House majority leader Tom DeLay contends that high crime rates and tragedies like the Columbine assault will continue as long as schools teach children "that they are nothing but glorified apes who have evolutionized [*sic*] out of some primordial soup of mud." . . .

Agreement with the hypothesis that popular religiosity is societally advantageous is not limited to those opposed to evolutionary science, or to conservatives. The basic thesis can be held by anyone who believes in a benign creator regardless of the proposed mode of creation, or the believer's social-political worldview. In broad terms the hypothesis that popular religiosity is socially beneficial holds that high rates of belief in a creator, as well as worship, prayer and other aspects of religious practice, correlate with lowering rates of lethal violence, suicide, non-monogamous sexual activity, and abortion, as well as improved physical health. Such faith-based, virtuous "cultures of life" are supposedly attainable if people believe that God created them for a special purpose, and follow the strict moral dictates imposed by religion. At one end of the spectrum are those who consider creator belief helpful but not necessarily critical to individuals and societies. At the other end the most ardent advocates consider persons and people inherently unruly and ungovernable unless they are strictly obedient to the creator. . . .

Religion and Prosperity

America's churches always reflect shifts in the broader culture. . . . The message that Jesus blesses believers with riches first showed up in the postwar years, at a time when Americans began to believe that greater comfort could be accessible to everyone, not just the landed class. But it really took off during the boom years of the 1990s, and has continued to spread ever since. This stitched-together, homegrown theology, known as the prosperity gospel, is not a clearly defined denomination, but a strain of belief that runs through the Pentecostal Church and a surprising number of mainstream evangelical churches, with varying degrees of intensity. In [one such] church, God is the "Owner of All the Silver and Gold," and with enough faith, any believer can access the inheritance. Money is not the dull stuff of hourly wages and bank-account statements, but a magical substance that comes as a gift from above. Even in these hard times, it is discouraged, in such churches, to fall into despair about the things you cannot afford. . . .

Many explanations have been offered for the housing bubble and subsequent crash: interest rates were too low; regulation failed; rising real-estate prices induced a sort of temporary insanity in America's middle class. But there is one explanation that speaks to a lasting and fundamental shift in American culture—a shift in the American conception of divine Providence and its relationship to wealth.

Hanna Rosin,
Atlantic Monthly, *December 2009.*

America as Morally Exceptional

The media gave favorable coverage to a report that children are hardwired towards, and benefit from, accepting the existence of a divine creator on an epidemiological and neuroscientific basis. Also covered widely was a Federal report that the economic growth of nations positively responds to high rates of belief in hell and heaven. Faith-based charities and education are promoted by the [George W.] Bush administration and religious allies and lobbies as effective means of addressing various social problems. The conservative Family Research Council proclaims, "believing that God is the author of life, liberty and the family, FRC promotes the Judeo-Christian worldview as the basis for a just, free and stable society." Towards the liberal end of the political spectrum [2000 Democratic] presidential candidate Al Gore supported teaching both creationism and evolution; his running mate Joe Lieberman asserted that belief in a creator is instrumental to "secure the moral future of our nation, and raise the quality of life for all our people," and [2004 Democratic] presidential candidate John Kerry emphasized his religious values in the latter part of his campaign.

With surveys showing a strong majority from conservative to liberal believing that religion is beneficial for society and for individuals, many Americans agree that their church-going nation is an exceptional, God blessed, "shining city on the hill" that stands as an impressive example for an increasingly skeptical world. But in the other developed democracies religiosity continues to decline precipitously and avowed atheists often win high office, even as clergies warn about adverse societal consequences if a revival of creator belief does not occur. . . .

Secularism and Societal Dysfunction

Among the developed democracies absolute belief in God, attendance of religious services and Bible literalism vary over a dozenfold, atheists and agnostics five fold, prayer rates four-fold, and acceptance of evolution almost twofold. Japan, Scandinavia, and France are the most secular nations in the west, the United States is the only prosperous first world nation to retain rates of religiosity otherwise limited to the second and third worlds. Prosperous democracies where religiosity is low (which excludes the U.S.) are referred to below as secular developed democracies.

Correlations between popular acceptance of human evolution and belief in and worship of a creator and Bible literalism are negative. The least religious nation, Japan, exhibits the highest agreement with the scientific theory, the lowest level of acceptance is found in the most religious developed democracy, the U.S.

A few hundred years ago rates of homicide were astronomical in Christian Europe and the American colonies. In all secular developed democracies a centuries-long trend has seen homicide rates drop to historical lows. . . . Despite a significant decline from a recent peak in the 1980s, the U.S. is the only prosperous democracy that retains high homicide rates, making it a strong outlier in this regard. Similarly, theistic Portugal also has rates of homicides well above the secular developed democracy norm. Mass student murders in schools are rare, and have subsided somewhat since the 1990s, but the U.S. has experienced many more than all the secular developed democracies combined. Other prosperous democracies do not significantly exceed the U.S. in rates of nonviolent and in non-lethal violent crime, and are often lower in this regard. The United States exhibits typical rates of youth suicide, which show little if any correlation with theistic factors in the prosperous democracies. The positive correlation between pro-theistic factors and juvenile mortality is remarkable, especially regarding absolute belief, and even prayer. Life spans tend to decrease as rates of religiosity rise, especially as a function of absolute belief. Denmark is the only exception. Unlike questionable small-scale epidemiological studies . . . , higher rates of religious affiliation, attendance, and prayer do not result in lower juvenile-adult mortality rates on a cross-national basis.

Although the late twentieth century STD [sexually transmitted disease] epidemic has been curtailed in all prosperous democracies, rates of adolescent gonorrhea infection remain six to three hundred times higher in the U.S. than in less theistic, pro-evolution secular developed democracies. . . . The U.S. also suffers from uniquely high adolescent and adult syphilis infection rates, which are starting to rise again as the microbe's resistance increases. . . . Increasing adolescent abortion rates show positive correlation with increasing belief and worship of a creator, and negative correlation with increasing non-theism and acceptance of evolution; again rates are uniquely high in the U.S. Claims that secular cultures aggravate abortion rates are therefore contradicted by the quantitative data. Early adolescent pregnancy and birth have dropped in the developed democracies, but rates are two to dozens of times higher in the U.S. where the decline has been more modest. Broad correlations between decreasing theism and increasing pregnancy and birth are present, with Austria and especially Ireland being partial exceptions. . . .

No "Shining City on the Hill"

In general, higher rates of belief in and worship of a creator correlate with higher rates of homicide, juvenile and early adult mortality, STD infection rates, teen pregnancy, and abortion in the prosperous democracies. The most theistic prosperous democracy, the U.S., is exceptional, but not in the manner [Benjamin] Franklin predicted. The United States is almost always the most dysfunctional of the developed democracies, sometimes spectacularly so, and almost always scores poorly. The view of the U.S. as a "shining city on the hill" to the rest of the world is falsified when it comes to basic measures of societal health. Youth suicide is an exception to the general trend because there is not a significant relationship between it and religious or secular factors. No democracy is known to have combined strong religiosity and popular denial of evolution with high rates of societal health. Higher rates of non-theism and acceptance of human evolution usually correlate with lower rates of dysfunction, and the least theistic nations are usually the least dysfunctional. None of the strongly secularized, pro-evolution democracies is experiencing high levels of measurable dysfunction. In some cases the highly religious U.S. is an outlier in terms of societal dysfunction from less theistic but otherwise socially comparable secular developed democracies. In other cases, the correlations are strongly graded, sometimes outstandingly so.

If the data showed that the U.S. enjoyed higher rates of societal health than the more secular, pro-evolution democracies, then the opinion that popular belief in a creator is strongly beneficial to national cultures would be supported. Although they are by no means utopias, the populations of secular democracies are clearly able to govern themselves and maintain societal cohesion. Indeed, the data examined in this study demonstrates that only the more secular, pro-evolution democracies have, for the first time in history, come closest to achieving practical "cultures of life" that feature low rates of lethal crime, juvenile-adult mortality, sex related dysfunction, and even abortion. The least theistic secular developed democracies such as Japan, France, and Scandinavia have been most successful in these regards. The non-religious, pro-evolution democracies contradict the dictum that a society cannot enjoy good conditions unless most citizens ardently believe in a moral creator. The widely held fear that a Godless citizenry must experience societal disaster is therefore refuted. Contradicting these conclusions requires demonstrating a positive link between theism and societal conditions in the first world with a similarly large body of data—a doubtful possibility in view of the observable trends.

> *"The church as an institution is really the only organized institution that these folks trust and that these folks see every day. It's the pastors and the people in these pews that are going after these people in Ward 7, in Milwaukee, in Harlem, on the lower East Side."*

Faith-Based Government Programs Have a Positive Impact on America

Aimee Welch

Until recently, religious organizations that worked with the government to provide charitable services for the needy were forced to become secular. Now, faith-based organizations are allowed to compete for government contracts without suppressing their religious nature. In the viewpoint that follows, Aimee Welch profiles one particular faith-based government program, called Faith Works, and tracks its successes and difficulties. Through an examination of this faith-based organization, Welch concludes that faith-based organizations should be fully embraced by the government and the people of the United States in order to adequately address both national and international concerns.

Aimee Welch, "Charitable Choice for Washington?" *Insight*, January 8, 2001, pp. 16–18. Reproduced by permission.

As you read, consider the following questions:

1. Why are religious organizations now allowed to compete for government contracts to provide welfare services without sacrificing their "religious character"?

2. What is Kevin Chavous's critique of methadone clinics?

3. What is the purpose of the organization Faith Works?

Democratic City Councilman Kevin Chavous grieves to see the long lines of heroin addicts awaiting government-subsidized fixes outside the methadone center in Ward 7, his slice of the troubled Southeast Washington neighborhood called Anacostia. "My ward has fallen prey to the problems of drug abuse," declares the councilman, who will be sworn for his third term in January 2001. "It's pretty intense. The methadone clinic is the worst example of drug treatment: You get rid of one addiction by starting another."

Chavous' constituents have complained of the effects of the methadone center on their neighborhoods, and he is looking for a fresh approach. "There is overwhelming public support for something new and innovative," he says. "A lot of the problems that we're having in the social-services arena aren't going to be solved by government alone."

Faith-Based Government Programs

And so Chavous has been talking with Bobby Polito, president of Faith Works, an organization whose faith-based model for rehabilitating inner-city drug addicts won national acclaim in New York City under Republican Mayor Rudy Giuliani and was replicated in 1999 in Milwaukee under the innovative leadership of Wisconsin Republican Gov. Tommy Thompson. . . .

Chavous says, "I've seen a lot of drug-treatment programs, but I've never seen anything as effective as Bobby's. I've been to New York; I've spoken with some of the clients."

The Faith Works therapy model—publicly funded to help homeless addicts in New York City beginning in 1993, and more recently expanded to help drug-addicted noncustodial fathers of children in the welfare system in Wisconsin—is uniquely holistic. Clients referred by churches, community groups and parole officers immediately are placed in work internships as they begin a "faith-enhanced" 12-step addiction-recovery program as well as a nutrition and exercise regimen. Gradually, education and work/skill training are added.

When participants are ready, they are encouraged to re-establish contact with their families and placed in private-sector jobs under close scrutiny by program counselors. Finally, Faith Works staff helps them locate independent housing and reintegrate into their communities. According to Polito, Faith Works has an 80 percent success rate with graduates staying drug- and alcohol-free, fully employed and in active relationships with their children.

"I think [bringing this program to Washington] would revolutionize our system in a way that people would not only be no longer dependent on drugs, but they would become self-sufficient," says Chavous. "We're in the midst of relooking at our whole approach to substance abuse, and I am going to at least have some language in the budget that we will vote on this spring that would allow for a look at [a faith-based] approach."

Historically, religious organizations that partnered with government to help the needy were forced to become secular. So religious organizations that considered spirituality to be essential to their effectiveness avoided such partnerships. But federal welfare-reform legislation passed in 1996 included a new "charitable-choice" provision that requires states to allow faith-based organizations to compete for government contracts to provide welfare services "on the same basis" as other providers without sacrificing their "religious character."

Evidence that Faith-Based Programs Change Lives

Ninety-six participants enrolled in a 14-session, 7-week faith-based welfare-to-work Neighbor to Neighbor [N2N] program developed and implemented by a Midwestern Catholic Charities agency. The participants were primarily Christian, single or divorced, White or African-American, women in their 30s who were living with from zero to three children. Of these 96 enrollees, 69 graduated from the program and had similar characteristics to the original enrollees. The 69 program graduates reported statistically significant gains in knowledge of community resources, awareness of personal strengths, making and achieving goals, budgeting, praying, and in their relationships with God as part of daily decision making. Most reported their lives changed from one that lacked direction and struggle to a sense of direction and a plan for their lives. Of the 69 N2N graduates in this study, 36 returned for the six-month follow-up group interview. All but two of the 36 reported achieving at least one of their four goals.

These findings show significant changes among the N2N participants and suggest that skills in meeting their spiritual needs, such as praying and having a relationship with God, may be as important as knowledge of community resources, budgeting, and goal setting. At least these achievements worked together so that participants report changed lives.

Source: Iris Phillips, et al., "Catholic Charities' Neighbor to Neighbor: Preliminary Findings of a Faith-Based Initiative," Journal of Religion and Spirituality in Social Work: Social Thought, *2008.*

Charitable-Choice Rules

Thus, faith-based organizations are guaranteed the freedom to display religious symbols, advance religious and moral concepts and use religious criteria for hiring staff, even when receiving federal funds, so long as they accept clients from any religious background, allow clients to opt out of religious activities and don't use government-contract funds for worship, doctrinal instruction or proselytizing. The provision also states that the government must provide a high-quality alternative source of assistance to any client who objects to a faith-based service provider.

Charitable-choice rules gradually have been extended by Congress to cover not only Department of Health and Human Services (HHS) welfare contracts but the Department of Labor's welfare-to-work programs, the HHS Community Services bloc grants and, as of October 2000, drug-treatment programs funded by the Substance Abuse and Mental Health Services Administration. "Since Republicans have taken Congress we have tried to open up the competition for federally funded programming contracts to faith-based organizations," says Kiki Kless, policy adviser to House Speaker Dennis Hastert of Illinois. "We don't feel they should be discriminated against."

Charitable Choice Expansion

On a recent visit to Washington, Polito was rushing between meetings with legislators concerning charitable-choice expansion and discussions with city officials to propose building an addiction-recovery center in Anacostia. But he paused long enough to down a cup of coffee and tell *Insight* how Faith Works is doing. His eyes flash as he dares any who object ad hoc to allowing religious groups to provide government services to come work in the inner city themselves. "In the last five months there have been eight homicides on the four corners of the block where I work. So, don't give me those oh-my-gosh-there's-a-7-a.m.-Bible-study-so-we've-got-to-shut-it-down objections. Something has to be done today, or yesterday. Not tomorrow. The fatherlessness, the breakdown of the inner city, kids running, kids having kids. . . . The church as an institution is really the only organized institution that these folks trust and that these folks see every day. It's the pastors and the people in these pews that are going after these people in Ward 7, in Milwaukee, in Harlem, on the lower East Side."

Determined to establish the legitimacy of his "demonstration model," Polito seeks evaluations of the program from an independent research firm and gets pro bono legal advice and accounting services from Milwaukee firms.

But what makes the program work, Polito contends, is community churches. He says pastors, through the women and children in their ministries, have helped link him to addicted fathers whom secular agencies couldn't even locate. "We come to a pastor as a resource. And how can I go to him and say, 'Give me $50 a day to house this guy?' They don't have those kinds of resources. This pastor's driving a bus all day because the church can't even support him, and I'm supposed to ask that the church support me? To do this kind of work? No way. No way. That's not going to happen."

He settles back in his chair. "We are a positive economic solution for the government. Over 80 percent of our men who are incarcerated are there because of their drug issues. Do you want to send them to a $50,000-a-year prison or a $12,000-a-year rehab that has no proven results? Everyone who comes into my centers in New York and Milwaukee, I guarantee them a job and we're averaging over $12 an hour, plus benefits. That's a $25,000-a-year job for a guy who has been addicted for 20-plus years and probably been incarcerated an average of about 10 or 12 years. Who does that? I don't go to the government and say we need job centers. . . . I go to my friends in the pews on Sunday who own companies, who own businesses. I ask them for more than money, I ask them for an involvement at some personal level."

Continuing the Partnership

Polito says, "I want to continue this public-private partnership. We did one in New York and that can be showcased because, like the song says, if you can do it in New York you can do it anywhere. . . . So after New York I would want to come here to Washington [D.C.]. Most people are not going to come to Milwaukee to see this, so if I could take legislators and administrators a mile from the Capitol and show them what we're doing I think we could showcase what can be done with a collaboration that would include the government, the faith community, the medical community, the business community."

Chavous is working hard to make that happen. "I think since it is new and people here haven't seen anything like it, we would have to do it on a pilot basis," he tells *Insight*. "But there's no doubt in my mind that once this program takes hold people will be clamoring for it to grow."

> *"Faith-based charities [have been given] a sweeping 'religious liberty' right to engage in employment bias in all federally funded programs."*

Faith-Based Government Programs Have a Negative Impact on America

Barry Lynn

Dissatisfaction with President Barack Obama's implementation of his newly named Council on Faith-Based and Neighborhood Partnerships has not been limited to the religious right that supported George W. Bush's programs. In the viewpoint that follows, Barry Lynn, executive director of Americans United for Separation of Church and State, an organization dedicated to preserving the constitutional separation of church and state in the United States, details his disappointment with Obama's policy decisions thus far and calls for the president to reassess his plans for faith-based programs. Lynn charges the president with failing to fulfill campaign promises regarding a new direction for faith-based initiatives and contends that Obama's policy has not

Barry Lynn, "Faith, Hope and Charity: Why President Obama's 'Faith-Based' Agenda Must Change," Huffington Post, February 4, 2010. Barry Lynn is Executive Director of Americans United for Separation of Church and State. Reproduced by permission of the publisher and author.

changed much from Bush's plan. Lynn maintains that without a dramatic policy shift, Obama's faith-based programs will continue to fail in the same manner as his predecessor's did.

As you read, consider the following questions:

1. What are some of the arguments that Lynn claims he made regarding the implementation of faith-based programs to ensure their success and the separation of church and state?

2. What troubles Lynn about certain council members appointed by President Barack Obama?

3. As stated by the author, how has the group World Vision discriminated against potential employees?

Speaking at the National Prayer Breakfast on February 4, [2010] President Barack Obama asserted that his administration has "turned the faith-based initiative around," implying that his policies represent a sharp break from past practices.

That's news to me. In fact, from where I'm sitting, the core of Obama's faith-based initiative looks pretty much identical to the deeply problematic one created by President George W. Bush. A few tweaks on the margins don't amount to real change.

Continuing Bush-Era Policies

One year after Obama announced his version of the faith-based office, civil rights and civil liberties groups such as mine are still fighting Bush-era battles over tax funding to religious groups that proselytize, job discrimination on religious grounds in public programs and lack of accountability. It's disheartening.

I am not a member of the president's 25-member Advisory Council on Faith-based and Neighborhood Partnerships,

the body Obama formed [in 2009] to examine these issues. But I did serve on a task force offering the Council advice on a range of questions.

During our deliberations, I often found myself on the other side from conservative religious activists who resisted even the most benign and reasonable rules that would safeguard the rights of taxpayers and the disadvantaged as well as help preserve the constitutional separation of church and state.

For example, I argued that all public funds that go to a house of worship to operate social services should be handled by a separately incorporated nonprofit—or at least be kept in a separate bank account so we can keep track of how the money is spent. A 2006 report by the General Accounting Office examined faith-based offices in several federal agencies and found a lack of oversight of these programs.

I also urged that publicly funded social services should not take place in a space where sectarian symbols or signs might make some disadvantaged people feel unwelcome. (Think of the homeless gay man who thinks of a large cross in a space providing dinner as the same icon wielded by Pastor Fred Phelps the last time he was in town to tell gays that they would be heading to hell.)

A Conflict of Interest

Conservative religious representatives on the Council disagreed. They want sectarian groups to have access to plenty of government money with very little (if any) meaningful accountability. That's the status quo; they like it.

Worse yet, some of the Council members appointed by President Obama are powerful religious lobbyists whose denominations and groups benefit handsomely from government funds. They include representatives from the U.S. Con-

Faith-Based Initiatives and Deregulation

When George W. Bush became president, he created the White House Office of Faith-Based and Community Initiatives and established Centers for Faith-Based Initiatives in five federal agencies: the Department of Health and Human Services, the Department of Housing and Urban Development, and departments of Labor, Justice, and Education. This was not Bush's first foray into the funding of faith-based groups. In 1997, when he was governor of Texas, the state legislature passed a program there allowing deregulation for faith-based reform schools. The legislature then passed a bill allowing the creation of alternative accreditation programs in which faith-based child-care centers could forego state licensing and instead receive accreditation from one of these newly created private agencies. Deregulation was an essential component of the faith-based initiative because it ensured that more faith-based providers would be eligible for government funds. And it substantially reduced health and safety requirements and oversight for these religious facilities.

Michele Tresler-Ulriksen, Humanist, *May/June 2009.*

ference of Catholic Bishops, Catholic Charities, the Union of Orthodox Jewish Congregations and the evangelical charity World Vision.

Our research in government databases indicates that Catholic Charities (including its various affiliates) has taken at least $521 million over the last 10 years. The Catholic bishops' conference has corralled $304.8 million over the same period, and World Vision has taken in $405.9 million. Orthodox Union–affiliated synagogues and Jewish schools have also benefited from millions in federal grants, though government reporting methods make the precise figure impossible to ascertain.

Wouldn't this be a conflict of interest by any ethical standard?

Obama Has Failed to Deliver

But, aside from the Council, other faith-based policies in the Obama administration are just as problematic. When Americans United [for Separation of Church and State, or AU] urged the Department of Justice (DOJ) to discontinue Bush-era funding for four fundamentalist groups that openly discriminate and proselytize, DOJ attorneys brushed aside the request. These organizations, they assured AU, had been told not to violate the law.

The DOJ, so far, has even refused to overturn a Bush-era memo that gives faith-based charities a sweeping "religious liberty" right to engage in employment bias in all federally funded programs.

All this is frustrating because we were promised something better. In a July 2008 Zanesville, Ohio, speech, Obama flatly promised to repeal Bush-era rules that let publicly funded faith-based groups discriminate in hiring on religious grounds. He also vowed to make sure that these groups do not proselytize the folks who come to them for help.

Obama could not have been clearer. "If you get a federal grant," he said, "you can't use that grant money to proselytize to the people you help and you can't discriminate against them—or against the people you hire—on the basis of their religion. Second, federal dollars that go directly to churches, temples, and mosques can only be used on secular programs. And we'll also ensure that taxpayer dollars only go to those programs that actually work."

Encouraging words. Too bad he hasn't acted on those promises, and billions of dollars in federal funds are still going out every day under Bush-era rules set up to evade long-standing civil rights and civil liberties protections.

Continuing to Subsidize Evangelicism

Don't think this doesn't matter in the real world or that it's all a theoretical spat among policy wonks obsessed with arcane Beltway [Washington] regulations. *The Global Post* recently ran a troubling story about World Vision, which received $281 million in government grants in 2008—yet offers full-time employment only to Christians who fit the group's creed.

The story makes it clear that people in other countries are being denied jobs in U.S.-funded programs because World Vision is discriminatory. As Torrey Olsen, World Vision's Senior Director for Christian Engagement, put it, "We do want to be witnesses to Jesus Christ by life, word, deed and sign." Fabiano Franz, another World Vision official, added, "We're very clear from the beginning about hiring Christians. It's not a surprise, so it's not discrimination."

Why is government—which is supported by taxpayers of many faiths and none—subsidizing such bias and evangelistic activity?

Dissatisfaction with Obama's inaction on this issue is widespread. On Feb. 4, [2010] 25 national religious and public policy organizations sent a letter to Obama, urging him to fix the faith-based initiative. The groups range from the American Association of University Women, the Human Rights Campaign and the National Association for the Advancement of Colored People to the American Jewish Committee, the Baptist Joint Committee for Religious Liberty and the United Methodist Church, General Board of Church and Society.

These groups have grown impatient with Obama, as have I, for leaving the odious Bush faith-based scheme in place unchanged.

Mr. President, this is not "change," and I am losing "hope." Please set your "faith-based" house in order. Shut down the

Faith-based Council and issue executive orders and regulations clearly banning hiring bias and proselytizing by faith-based groups that take public funds.

> *"If God himself gave human beings free will—the choice to love him or not, to obey him or not—then no believer should try to force another to confess a faith."*

Politics and Religion Should Be Separate

Jon Meacham

With a federal judge ruling that the National Day of Prayer was unconstitutional, the debate over the role of religion and politics was thrust into the spotlight. Christians and conservatives, like former Alaska governor Sarah Palin, try to convince the public that religion and politics should intermingle because our Founding Fathers were believers. Meacham argues that Palin's argument is shaky because even though the Founders were believers, their greatest legacy was creating a culture in which the secular and religious could coexist separately. According to the author, even Jesus himself declared a separation between the church and state. Jon Meacham is the editor of Newsweek *magazine.*

Jon Meacham, "The Religious Case for Church-State Separation," *Newsweek*, April 23, 2010. Reproduced by permission.

As you read, consider the following questions:

1. What two men called for a "hedge or wall of separation between the garden of the church and the wilderness of the world"?

2. According to the author, with whom did the idea of separation of church and state begin?

3. Why does the author say that a Christian nation is a "theological impossibility"?

Here we go again. On April 15 [2010] a federal judge in Wisconsin ruled that the National Day of Prayer, slated for May 6, was unconstitutional. The usual voices have been heard rising in objection ([former Alaska governeror] Sarah Palin and [evangelist] Franklin Graham among them) and, proving yet again that President [Barack] Obama is no radical, the administration announced its own plans to challenge the decision. One can make a reasonable case that the weight of custom puts the fairly banal idea of an occasionless, generic day of prayer (how many of you even knew that we have had such a day every year since 1952?) on the safe side of the Establishment Clause. But the right is, as ever, taking things a beat too far. Lest anyone try to convince you that God should be separated from the state, Palin said, our Founding Fathers, they were believers.

Governor Palin's history is rather shaky. Religious liberty—the freedom to worship as one chooses, or not to worship—is a central element of the American creed. Yes, many of the Founders were believing, observant Christians. But to think of them as apostles in knee breeches or as passionate evangelicals is a profound misreading of the past. In many ways their most wondrous legacy was creating the foundations of a culture of religious diversity in which the secular and the religious could live in harmony, giving faith a role in the life

Americans Want a President with Strong Religious Beliefs

	Agree %	Disagree %	DK %
August, 2008	72	25	3 = 100
August, 2007	69	27	4 = 100
August, 2004	70	26	4 = 100
Republican	86	12	2 = 100
Democrat	68	29	3 = 100
Independent	66	31	3 = 100
White Protestant	83	15	2 = 100
Evangelical	90	8	2 = 100
Mainline	76	21	3 = 100
Black Protestant	80	18	2 = 100
White Catholic	77	19	4 = 100
Unaffiliated	36	62	2 = 100

Note: Survey participants were asked whether they agreed or disagreed with the following statement, "It's important to me that a president have strong religious beliefs."

TAKEN FROM: Pew Forum on Religion & Public Life, Results from the 2008 Annual Religion and Public Life Survey, August 21, 2008.

of the nation in which it could shape us without strangling us. On the day George Washington left Philadelphia to take command of the Continental Army, the Rev. William Smith preached a sermon at the city's Christ Church, saying: "Religion and liberty must flourish or fall together in America. We pray that both may be perpetual."

Religious Argument for Separation

Arguments about the connection between religion and politics, church and state, have surely been perpetual. The civil and legal cases against religious coercion are well known: human freedom extends to one's conscience, and by abolishing religious tests for office or mandated observances, Americans have successfully created a climate—a free market, if you will—in which religion can take its stand in the culture and in the country without particular help or harm from the government.

There is a religious case against state involvement with matters of faith, too. Long before Thomas Jefferson, Roger Williams, the founder of Rhode Island, called for a "hedge or wall of separation between the garden of the church and the wilderness of the world," believing, with the Psalmist [David, composer of the Book of Psalms in the Hebrew Bible], that human beings were not to put their trust in princes. The principalities and powers of a fallen world represented and still represent a corrupting threat to religion: too many rulers have used faith to justify and excuse all manner of evil.

The idea of separation began, in fact, with Jesus. Once, when the crowds were with him and wanted to make him a king, he withdrew and hid. Before Pilate, Jesus was explicit: "My kingdom is not of this world," he said. Later in the New Testament, Paul argues that God shows no partiality among nations or peoples, meaning nations cannot claim blessed status, and says that "there is neither Jew nor Greek, there is neither slave nor free man, there is neither male nor female; for you are all one in Christ Jesus," which means the Lord God of Hosts is concerned with larger matters than whether one is an American or a Norwegian. A Christian nation, then, is a theological impossibility, and faith coerced is no faith at all, only tyranny. If God himself gave human beings free will—the choice to love him or not, to obey him or not—then no believer should try to force another to confess a faith.

Let Religion Take Its Own Stand

The Founders understood this. Washington said we should give "to bigotry no sanction, to persecution no assistance"; according to the 1797 Treaty of Tripoli, ratified by the Senate and signed by John Adams, "the government of the United States is not, in any sense, founded on the Christian religion."

Jefferson said that his statute for religious freedom in Virginia was "meant to comprehend, within the mantle of its protection, the Jew and the Gentile, the Christian and the Mohammedan [Muslim], the Hindoo and Infidel of every denomination." There are many precedents for the National Day of Prayer, but serious believers, given the choice between a government-sanctioned religious moment and the perpetuation of a culture in which religion can take its own stand, free from the corruptions of the world, should always choose the garden of the church over the wilderness of the world. It is, after all, what Jesus did.

| "*The largest, deepest issues require religious engagement for political resolution to become possible.*"

Politics and Religion Cannot Be Separated

Hunter R. Rawlings III

Religion is a necessary and inextricable aspect of politics and public life in the United States, argues former Cornell University president Hunter R. Rawlings III in the following viewpoint. Rawlings examines the position of religion in the political sphere in both a historical and contemporary context. He contends that religious ideals and beliefs have in the past offered and will continue to provide important insight into some of the most pressing issues the United States has ever faced, including slavery and abortion. Religion, the author concludes, can offer moral guidance where science and reason fail and can comfort a nation in its most dire times.

As you read, consider the following questions:

1. What three prominent issues does Rawlings note as being revelatory of the power of religion in the public sphere?

Hunter R. Rawlings III, "Lecture: What Place Do Religious Ideas Have in American Politics?" Woodrow Wilson Center, May 11, 2006. Reproduced by permission of the author.

2. As stated by the author, when is religion most effective publicly?

3. What role should religion play in the abortion debate, according to Rawlings?

On March 4, 1865, Abraham Lincoln delivered the most moving and probably the most significant speech in American history, his Second Inaugural Address. Lincoln used his presidential platform to give an anguished rumination on the purposes of the Almighty and the consequences for Americans, in both North and South, of practicing slavery. The Second Inaugural is, as many have pointed out, essentially a sermon. Its biblical, indeed prophetic, rhetoric has had a powerful effect upon all subsequent Presidential speechmaking, which struggles, never successfully, to emulate it. In spite of our constitutional separation of church and state, America's chief executives rarely deliver a major address without a direct appeal to God. . . .

Religion Returns to the Public Square

Even when Americans deny the state establishment of any religion, prohibit religious tests for public office, and never so much as mention God in their Constitution; and even when leaders with such consciously antisectarian views as Ezra Cornell and A.D. White found a center for scientific thought and reason [Cornell University], what has been called the first "truly American university," religion is omnipresent. Today, in the midst of what history will probably call "the third Great Awakening," we Americans are seeing a massive movement of religion back into the public square, particularly in the crucial arenas of politics and education. Abortion, stem cell research, and Intelligent Design are just three of the prominent issues revealing the power of religion in local school boards, colleges and universities, municipal governments, state legislatures, and the Congress and the White House. [In April 2006] 55 Democrats in the House of Representatives issued a joint statement clarifying the central role Catholicism plays in their policy making. President [George W.] Bush makes constant reference to the faith that governs his life and thought, both public and private.

If corpses can do such a thing, my favorite Founder, James Madison, is turning in his Virginia grave. Madison sincerely believed that, together with his political partner Thomas Jefferson, he had once and for all separated church and state in America in the 1780s and early '90s. In drafting the revolutionary clause on freedom of conscience in Virginia's Declaration of Rights, in defeating Patrick Henry's bill for a religious tax by publishing the Memorial and Remonstrance against Religious Assessments, in pushing Jefferson's Bill for Establishing Religious Freedom through the Virginia Assembly, in helping to author the Constitution, and in drafting the First Amendment, Madison made separation of Church and State his first principle. Far from supporting Patrick Henry's and George Washington's belief that state support of religion would improve the morals of American society, Madison argued, adamantly and repeatedly, that yoking Church and State together had been disastrous throughout history for both religion and the body politic. To use religion as an instrument of civil policy is, in Madison's words, "an unhallowed perversion of the means of salvation." . . .

Impossible to Separate

And yet it has proven impossible to separate church and state completely. Why is that? "Politics is in large part a function of culture"; and "at the heart of culture is religion," [U.S. clergyman] Richard John Neuhaus wrote three decades ago, as he worried that the public square had become "naked," that is, shorn of religious belief and values. Neuhaus, as it turned out, had nothing to fear. But Madisonians do. Evangelical Protestantism has in recent years become ever more potent in American public life, while the voices of secular humanists become ever more strident in their reaction to religious rhetoric. This is a badly polarized state of affairs, as we have recently seen in national debates over the case of Terry Schiavo[1], abortion, stem cell research, and the opposition of Darwinism and Intelligent Design. What is the right way out of this polarized situation?

Let us begin by acknowledging that Madison was wrong: the state *must* take cognizance of religion: it is too important a source of ideas and values to ignore or to privatize completely. Religion shapes most Americans' values, aspirations, beliefs, in sum, their identities. The history of this country reflects the simultaneous development of grassroots democracy and evangelical Protestantism. The two have gone hand in hand, often reinforcing one another. The problem is that the absolutist tendencies of religion frequently become incompatible with democratic pluralism and the need for give and take in politics. As [American theologian] Reinhold Niebuhr warned, "The religious imagination is as impatient with the compromises, relativities and imperfections of historic society as with the imperfections of individual life." How can we ensure, then, that religion will inform and improve policy debate, but not polarize? And equally, if not more importantly, how can Americans protect their faiths from becoming political religions, "unhallowed perversions of the means of salvation," to use Madison's memorable phrase? These are, in my view, two of the most pressing questions we Americans confront today. . . .

Religion's Role in Public Policy

Many American Christians find the intense political engagement of some Christian churches not only embarrassing, but an affront to their conception of the church as a spiritual

---

1. The case of Terry Schiavo, a woman who had been in a vegetative state for years, was the subject of a hot national debate in 2005 when her husband's request to have her life support discontinued was legally opposed by Terry's parents.

home, not a partisan political actor. As Niebuhr showed, public demonstration of piety can corrupt private faith by transferring religious rhetoric to the political realm, thus lowering and cheapening it. It is bad enough when religious leaders make political pronouncements; it is worse when government leaders use the church for partisan advantage. Niebuhr wrote that "The religion which is socially most useful is one which can maintain a stubborn indifference to immediate ends and thus give the ethical life of man that touch of the absolute without which all morality is finally reduced to a decorous but essentially unqualified self-assertiveness. The paradox of religion is that it serves the world best when it maintains its high disdain for the world's values. . . . Its assets easily become moral liabilities when it compounds the pure idealism of Jesus with the calculated practicalities of the age and attempts to give the resultant compromise the prestige of absolute authority."

Religion is most effective publicly, then, not when it joins with the state and speaks prescriptively, but when it acts in what Niebuhr called its prophetic role. Faith can be a great moral force to reform society when government and science fail, as they often do. Madison's beloved Constitution did not end slavery, the Abolitionists and then Lincoln did. Civil rights finally came for African Americans partly because secularists called for it, but primarily because Martin Luther King and his Southern Baptist colleagues demanded it on religious and moral grounds. It takes a wake-up call from Catholic Bishops to get Americans to confront the problem of serious poverty in our midst, even if only briefly. In the same way, we can be certain that the issue of abortion will not be solved on the basis of scientific definitions and legal procedures alone. Science and the law have little to tell us about the meaning of life. That is the domain of religious sensibility and moral sensitivity.

Religious Dialogue Needed

The religious ideas of masses of Americans have been shielded from the aspects of modern thought that have led so many scientists and social scientists away from religion. Perhaps critical debate would encourage popular faiths to be more consistent with modern standards of plausibility, more resistant to the manipulation of politicians belonging to any party, and more accepting of the wisdom in the sharp separation between church and state. Where, after all did we get liberal religion? We got it out of orthodox religion. Especially did the great biblical scholars of the eighteenth and nineteenth century provide the cognitive context for a variety of liberalized religious faiths, including the capacity of many Christians to absorb the Darwinian revolution in science. Religious dialogue has been vital to the intellectual and political history of the North Atlantic West for centuries, until twentieth-century secularists complacently assumed religion was on the way out and ceased to engage it critically.

David A. Hollinger,
Representations, *Winter 2008.*

Religion and the Abortion Debate

Abortion is the most divisive domestic issue afflicting America today. We academics have consistently misunderstood and undervalued religious arguments about abortion, much to our own and the nation's detriment. Our inability to appreciate the role of religious conviction in discussing abortion is probably the single greatest cause of our diminished role in public policy debate. Most academics are secular humanists. That is neither surprising nor especially noteworthy, but academic disdain for religion, specifically for Christianity, is noteworthy, and it has unfortunate consequences. Such disdain diminishes the capacity of many academics to understand American culture and politics, and thus lessens their influence in the public square. It is thought-provoking to note that, although it is liberals who have moved America to an ever more inclusive definition of humanity and human rights over the past century, it is now anti-abortion advocates who are calling for expanding our conception of human life. This is the religious voice speaking, like Abolitionists in the nineteenth century, while, on the other side, liberal academics seem often to accord more respect to animal rights arguments than to appeals for the "rights of the fetus." By the same token, I would sympathize more with arguments from faith about the beginning of life if those who make them showed more interest in moral arguments against ending life. Whatever side one is on in the abortion debate, or in the debate over the death penalty, two things appear clear to me: religious views will play a large role in the eventual outcome; and each side needs to show greater respect to the moral basis for the other's arguments.

How Religion Can Inform Politics

When I ask myself how religion should inform politics, I keep returning to Madison and Lincoln. Madison spent a lifetime trying to ensure that this country would avoid Europe's long history of religious conflict by separating church and state. Our Constitution and our Bill of Rights do as much as legal documents can do to assure his success. But his could only be a partial victory, because religion cannot long be kept out of the public square in this or any other country. The largest, deepest issues require religious engagement for political resolution to become possible. This country's greatest crisis, the final confrontation over slavery, needed, in the end, religious understanding, a national benediction after a national tragedy. Presiding over civil war and incalculable suffering, Lincoln composed for his second inaugural address a national sermon. Though he found it impossible in spite of great effort to believe in personal salvation. And though he did not join a church, Lincoln read the Bible nearly every day as a source of strength and of powerful poetic language. Borrowing the language of the Old Testament prophets, and of Christian mercy, he tried to help his fellow countrymen understand the meaning of the Civil War in their history.

Periodical Bibliography

The following articles have been selected to supplement the diverse views presented in this chapter.

Christianity Today	"Faith Is Not a Freak Show," August 2008.
Economist	"The Lesson from America," November 3, 2007.
D.J. Grothe	"Seven Reasons Obama's Faith-Based Initiative Is Wrong," *Free Inquiry*, June/July 2009.
Mollie Ziegler Hemingway	"Faith-Based Double Standards," *Wall Street Journal*, September 11, 2009.
Daniel Horowitz and Ruth Mitchell	"Safeguarding Religious Liberty in Charitable Choice and Faith-Based Initiatives," *Free Inquiry*, June/July 2009.
Jane Lampman	"Obama Plans Faith-Based Initiatives," *Christian Science Monitor*, January 5, 2009.
Thomas W. Merrill	"Distracted by Religion: On Doing Bioethics in Public," *Perspectives on Political Science*, Spring 2009.
Barack Obama	"One Nation . . . Under God?" *Sojourners Magazine*, November 2006.
Katha Pollitt	"Onward, Secular Soldiers," *Nation*, September 24, 2007.
Stephanie Simon	"In Political Ads, Christian Left Mounts Sermonic Campaigns," *Wall Street Journal*, July 3, 2009.
Andrew Stephen	"How Would Jesus Vote?" *New Statesman*, February 4, 2008.
Jay Tolson	"A Complex Role for Religion," *U.S. News & World Report*, July 7, 2008.

**OPPOSING
VIEWPOINTS®
SERIES**

CHAPTER 3

What Should Be Done to Accommodate Religious Freedom in America?

Chapter Preface

In the late 1990s Muslim cab drivers at the Minneapolis–St. Paul International Airport began refusing to transport customers who obviously carried alcoholic beverages. The transparent duty-free bags used to hold bottles of liquor alerted these drivers that a patron possessed alcohol, and the cabbies would simply tell the potential fares to hail another available taxi. According to the cab drivers, the transportation of alcohol is a punishable sin under Islam, and therefore they believed they had the duty to deny service based on their faith. What the cabbies found, though, was that when they passed up a fare, they had to circle back through the cab stand lines and take up position at the end of the taxi queue to await another fare. In 2000, the Muslim drivers began complaining that it was unfair to be banished to the end of the line because they were exercising a religious right. The airport transportation authority disagreed.

By 2006, the number of Muslim cab drivers at the Minneapolis–St. Paul Airport had grown significantly. Three-quarters of the nine hundred cabbies working the airport run were Muslim, and airport spokesperson Patrick Hogan told the Associated Press that these drivers were turning down an average of three fares per day because of the alcohol issue. Hogan added that the problem was no longer just affecting the drivers but that it had "slowly grown over the years to the point that it's become a significant customer service issue." The airport's solution was to allow Muslim cabbies to have their taxi-in-service light bear a different color from the other drivers so that customers would know which vehicles to avoid if they happened to be carrying alcohol.

The two-light proposal, however, upset many observers. Daniel Pipes, a political commentator and outspoken critic of radical Islam, argued that providing Muslim drivers with a special privilege was a dangerous precedent. As he warns, "Why stop with alcohol? Muslim taxi drivers in several countries already balk at allowing seeing-eye dogs in their cars. Future demands could include not transporting women with exposed arms or hair, homosexuals, and unmarried couples." The local area public also disparaged the accommodation. In October 2006, the airport rejected the two-light solution. Metropolitan Airports Commission (MAC) executive director Jeff Hamiel stated that the proposal had been thwarted because "it is clear that its implementation could have unintended and significant negative impacts on the taxi industry as a whole." The MAC also imposed new regulations requiring all cabbies to pick up legitimate fares or risk losing their licenses. The Muslim cabbies tried to fight this restriction in court but finally lost their appeals battle in 2008.

Abdifatah Abdi, who told local reporters that he spoke for an association of cabdrivers, condemned the decision and the MAC commissioners' stipulations. "You are deciding the livelihood of 600 drivers and their families," Abdi said. "Say no to discrimination. Say yes to justice for the weak." As this incident in Minnesota demonstrates, the United States—a nation that promises religious freedom—is still struggling to determine the extent and boundaries of that liberty. In the following chapter, commentators and critics debate other ways in which the United States might accommodate religious practice under the laws of the land.

| "Students who want to do serious study of Western civilization need to know the Bible."

Bible Classes Should Be Offered in Public Schools

William R. Mattox Jr.

In the viewpoint that follows, William R. Mattox Jr. claims that the Bible should be taught in public schools. According to Mattox, a lack of understanding of Bible stories, words, and characters negatively affects secular students who will undoubtedly encounter biblical references in classic literature and the arts. In addition, Mattox asserts that a greater knowledge of the Bible will improve students' comprehension of Christianity's influence on history. According to Mattox, many academics support the teaching of the Bible—in a nondevotional manner—to aid public school students in becoming more aware of these allusions that pervade Western culture. William R. Mattox Jr. writes for USA Today, *a daily national newspaper.*

As you read, consider the following questions:

1. Why does Mattox believe that knowledge of the Bible is necessary to understand the role of Martin Luther King Jr. in the civil rights movement?

William R. Mattox Jr., "Teach the Bible? Of Course," *USA Today*, August 17, 2009. Reproduced by permission of the author.

2. As Mattox relates, what fact did a 2008 study published in *Sociological Quarterly* discover?

3. According to the author, what three states have recently passed legislation to offer Bible literacy classes as elective courses in public high schools?

Having held a successful "beer-and-nuts summit" to defuse the volatile issue of race in public life, President [Barack] Obama now needs to hold a "wine-and-bread summit" to tackle the equally volatile issue of religion in public schools.

Because as millions of American children return to the classroom this month [August 2009], most public schools do not know how to handle the delicate issue of what to teach students about the Bible. Just ask the Texas Board of Education, which is mired in a contentious fight over how textbooks should characterize Christianity's influence on American history.

Familiar Battle Lines

The battle lines in the Texas shootout are familiar: One side wants to purge public schools of almost any respectful mention of religion, while the other wants the Bible to be given even more reverence in the classroom than that afforded great Americans like, say, Martin Luther King Jr.

Given this stark divide, it's easy to see why some educators might be tempted to skirt this topic. Yet, to its credit, the Texas Board of Education is soldiering on, knowing that you can't effectively explore American history without teaching about the Rev. King, and that you can't teach about the civil rights leader without helping students understand the meaning and power of his frequent references to "the Promised Land" and other scriptural metaphors, verses and concepts.

Hopefully, Texas and other states can strike the right balance—and raise our nation's biblical literacy levels without engaging in religious indoctrination of one kind or another.

For while people on different sides will object to the Bible being misused in the classroom, all of us on all sides ought to object to the Bible being ignored in the classroom.

"Students who want to do serious study of Western civilization need to know the Bible," says Barbara Newman, Northwestern University professor of English, Religion and Classics. "They need to know the Bible, even if they do not believe the Bible."

Support for Bible Literacy

Harvard professor Robert Kiely, for one, agrees. In 2006, he participated in an academic survey of professors from many of America's leading universities—including Yale, Princeton, Brown, Rice, California-Berkeley and Stanford. The survey—commissioned by the Bible Literacy Project, which promotes academic Bible study in public schools—found an overwhelming consensus among top professors that incoming college students need to be well-versed in the stories, themes and words of the Bible.

"If a student doesn't know any Bible literature, he or she will simply not understand whole elements of [William] Shakespeare, [Philip] Sidney, [Edmund] Spenser, [John] Milton, [Alexander] Pope, [William] Wordsworth. One could go on and on and on," Kiely told Concordia professor Marie Wachlin and her research team.

"Knowledge of the Bible can be a key to unlocking other subjects . . . especially literature, art, music and social studies," say Chuck Stetson, co-editor of the visually stunning high school textbook *The Bible and Its Influence,* and founder of the Bible Literacy Project.

And knowledge of the Bible can be a key to understanding much of today's pop culture. Like Stephen Colbert's irreverent humor on Comedy Central. Or Jim Carrey's screwball spirituality in *Bruce Almighty.* Or the devilishly clever title of the band White Stripes' release, *Get Behind Me Satan.*

Not surprisingly, students growing up in non-religious homes are often behind the curve. "Many of my students are quite secular and have very little knowledge of the Bible," Northwestern's Newman says. "This is a major disadvantage."

Indeed, Newman says that trying to appreciate biblical allusions in literature without an underlying knowledge of Scripture is like trying to appreciate a good joke when someone has to explain the punch line. You might eventually "get" the joke, she says, but by the time you do, "it's not funny anymore."

Interestingly, a 2008 study published in *Sociological Quarterly* found that regular church attendance positively affected students' grade point averages. And while lead researcher Jennifer Glanville of the University of Iowa attributed much of this effect to the social and psychological benefits of being enmeshed in a wider community of like-minded peers and adults, some of this effect might also be explained by the greater biblical literacy young people typically acquire by attending church.

A Non-devotional Approach to Bible Studies

To stem the decline of biblical literacy, three states—Georgia, Texas and Tennessee—have passed laws in recent years calling for public high schools to offer elective courses that teach the Bible "in an objective and non-devotional manner with no attempt to indoctrinate students" (as Georgia's law puts it).

In addition, some educators have sought to shore up world religion units that too often, in Kiely's words, "go rapidly over all the Quran in one week and all of the Bible in two days."

Though these are welcome developments, Obama could give them a real boost by holding a wine-and-bread summit at the White House to legitimize Bible courses in public schools. And in a strange sort of way, such an initiative ought to please everyone.

For while true believers will no doubt hope that elective Bible courses might whet students' appetites for more, non-believers can take solace in the fact that if schools don't start doing a better job of teaching students about the Bible, many parents who want their kids to be high achievers just might start taking them to church.

> *"Rather than single out the Bible . . . for special courses in our public schools, it would be better to incorporate objective discussion about religion into the curriculum when it is appropriate."*

Bible Classes Should Not Be Offered in Public Schools

Michael Jinkins

Americans United for Separation of Church and State is a nonpartisan organization devoted to preserving the constitutional separation between church and state. The following viewpoint is an editorial from the organization's magazine Church & State. *In it, the author, Michael Jinkins, contends that teaching Bible classes in public schools is wrongheaded. Jinkins claims that there are so many versions of the Bible—each with its own supporting sect—that deciding on a standard text would be impossible and likely cause conflict between sectarian groups as well as between believers and secularists. In the Jinkins's opinion, it is better to allow teachers of English and history to clarify references to the Bible and its pervasive influence on civilization in a nonproselytizing manner rather than force public institutions to adopt religion-centered courses.*

Michael Jinkins, "Constitutional Literacy: Why American Schools Don't Need Bible Classes," *Church & State*, vol. 60, May 2007, p. 13. Copyright © 1947–2010 Americans United for Separation of Church and State. Reproduced by permission of the author.

As you read, consider the following questions:

1. Why does the publication say that "there is no such thing as 'the Bible'?"

2. According to *Church & State* the online *World Christian Encyclopedia* (2001), as cited by the author, how many Christian denominations exist worldwide?

3. What does the fighting between the National Council on Bible Curriculum in Public Schools and the Bible Literacy Project demonstrate, according to *Church & State*?

The campaign to institute Bible classes in public schools is picking up steam.

Boston University religion professor Stephen Prothero has thrown gasoline on the fire with the publication of his recent book *Religious Literacy: What Every American Needs to Know— and Doesn't*. In the book, Prothero asserts that classes on the Bible should be mandatory in American high schools. David Van Biema, a *Time* magazine religion writer, endorsed the idea, although he stopped short of saying the classes should be mandatory.

Prothero is getting a bit of a media buzz. He has placed op-eds here and there and even appeared on Oprah Winfrey's program to plug his book. Legislatures in at least five states, Texas being the largest, are considering classes about the Bible. Legislation has already passed in Georgia.

It's time to slow down and take a look at some hard questions this approach raises.

Which Version Should Be Used?

First off, there is no such thing as "the Bible." Rather, there are translations of that work—lots of them. Most people know there are differences between the Bibles used by Protestants and Catholics. That's just the beginning. Christians use many different translations. One online site listed more than 100 different translations in English alone. The differences among these versions are not minor, as some might argue. People quibble over every word and feel strongly about the accuracy of one translation over others. Which version are we to use in public schools?

The number of Bible translations should not surprise anyone. There are, after all, many variations of Christianity. The Web site www.adherents.com, quoting a 2001 edition of the *World Christian Encyclopedia*, claims there are more than 33,000 denominations of Christianity worldwide.

To be fair, we should point out that many of these groups are small splinter spin-offs of larger bodies. The fact that such splintering occurs as frequently as it does underscores the point that people feel passionately about faith and the holy books that they believe support their beliefs.

We cannot simply gloss over this issue and pretend that it won't be relevant. In fact, our country has a long history of arguing about the Bible and how it ought to be used in public schools. This issue sparked violence between Catholics and Protestants in some parts of the country in the mid 19th century. Some state supreme courts, noting the infighting, blocked public schools from using the Bible in a devotional manner prior to the U.S. Supreme Court's landmark ruling in this area in 1963 [in *Abington School District v. Schempp*].

Consequences of Sectarian Squabbling

But even that hasn't stopped the squabbling. Debates about how to teach even supposedly objective courses drag on. The North Carolina-based National Council on Bible Curriculum in Public Schools is offering a curriculum that Americans United argues is best left in a conservative Sunday School. Supporters of the National Council frequently take potshots at the rival curriculum offered by the Bible Literacy Project.

The Bible Literacy Project's textbook, *The Bible and Its Influence*, is certainly better than what the National Council of-

Best Place for Teaching Faith

Would you want public school teachers interpreting the Bible for your kids? In some schools teachers may promote the Bible because they are believing Christians. In other schools teachers with a secular humanist bent will undermine its legitimacy. The best place for faith to be taught to kids is in the home, church, and private schools.

Christopher Ruddy, Newsmax,
March 28, 2007. www.newsmax.com.

fers, although it too has serious flaws. The ironic thing is, both of these organizations are coming from a mindset that could fairly be called conservative. Yet they disagree bitterly on how the Bible is to be taught in schools.

Battles like this could erupt all over the nation. Imagine you are one of the few progressive Christians, Jews or nonbelievers living in a small town in Alabama. In an area like this, where fundamentalism holds sway and many science teachers are afraid to even mention the word "evolution," what type of Bible course will your school offer? Will it be objective and balanced—or will the local band of [evangelical leader] James Dobson devotees apply enough pressure to make sure the class is taught to their liking?

The Objective Discussion Solution

There is a better way. Rather than single out the Bible, the religious text of only some believers, for special courses in our public schools, it would be better to incorporate objective discussion about religion into the curriculum when it is appropriate.

This could be done in many different types of classes. An English teacher discussing John Steinbeck's *East of Eden* could point out that the title comes from Genesis and discuss the biblical allusions in the work. An art history class could discuss the ways biblical themes have appeared in various paintings. History teachers could talk about the role—positive and negative—that religion played in events like the Civil War and the struggle for civil rights.

As long as teachers don't use these moments to proselytize—overtly or covertly—academic needs, religious pluralism and the Constitution will all be respected.

This approach is to be preferred because it rests more on the mere transmission of factual information and less on interpretation. No matter how we try to avoid it, a class focusing solely on the Bible requires instructors to wade into theological thickets. There is too much disagreement in American society on what the Bible is, how it is to be read and which version is to be read to avoid problems.

The last thing this country needs is another front in the "culture war." Public school courses "about" the Bible will provide that—especially if they are mandated. There are better ways to teach about religion in public schools. We ought to pursue them instead.

I *"The rights of medical conscience need
to be expanded and made explicit."*

Medical Practitioners
Should Be Protected
by Conscience Clauses

Wesley J. Smith

*In the viewpoint that follows, Wesley J. Smith argues that the
medical and legal institutions of the United States are becoming
increasingly hostile toward doctors who refuse to commit acts
that violate their moral codes. Smith contends that modern
medical practice is being coerced by lawmakers who believe
patients' rights supersede doctors' rights in all instances—even
when doctors are asked to go against their religious beliefs or to
perform lethal acts (such as assisting in euthanasia) that they
find unnecessary. Smith believes that the conscience clauses in
medical contracts should be binding and not deprive doctors of
their right to decline to take part in medical procedures that they
find objectionable on moral grounds. Wesley J. Smith is a senior
fellow in bioethics and human rights at the Discovery Institute,*

Wesley J. Smith, "Pulling the Plug on the Conscience Clause," *First Things: A Monthly
Journal of Religion and Public Life*, December 2009, pp. 41–44. Copyright © 2009 Institute on Religion and Public Life. All rights reserved. Reproduced by permission.

a nonpartisan public policy think tank. He is also the author of Forced Exit: Euthanasia, Assisted Suicide and the New Duty to Die *and other works.*

As you read, consider the following questions:

1. What was the outcome of the circuit court case of *Stormans Inc. v. Selecky*, as Smith describes it?

2. What does the author see as an ominous outcome of the Australian Abortion Law Reform Act of 2008?

3. According to Smith, what was one of the first public acts of the Obama administration in regard to medical conscience mandates?

Over the past fifty years, the purposes and practices of medicine have changed radically. Where medical ethics was once life-affirming, today's treatments and medical procedures increasingly involve the legal taking of human life. The litany is familiar: More than one million pregnancies are extinguished each year in the United States, thousands late-term. Physician-assisted suicide is legal in Oregon, Washington, and, as this is written [in 2009], Montana via a court ruling (currently on appeal to the state supreme court). One day, doctors may be authorized to kill patients with active euthanasia, as they do already in the Netherlands, Belgium, and Luxembourg.

Disturbing Ethical Trends

The trend toward accepting the termination of some human lives as a normal part of medicine is accelerating. For example, ten or twenty years from now, the physician's tools may include embryonic stem cells or products obtained from cloned embryos and fetuses gestated for that purpose, making physicians who provide such treatments complicit in the life destruction required to obtain the modalities. Medical and bioethics journals energetically advocate a redefinition of death to include a diagnosis of persistent vegetative state so that these living patients—redefined as dead—may be used for organ harvesting and medical experimentation. More radical bioethicists and mental-health professionals even suggest that patients suffering from BIID (body-integrity identity disorder), a terrible compulsion to become an amputee, should be treated by having healthy limbs removed, just as transsexuals today receive surgical sexual reassignment.

The ongoing transformation in the methods and ethics of medicine raises profound moral questions for doctors, nurses, pharmacists, and others who believe in the traditional virtues of Hippocratic medicine that proscribe abortion and assisted suicide and compel physicians to "do no harm." To date, this hasn't been much of a problem, as society generally accommodates medical conscientious objection. The assisted-suicide laws of Oregon and Washington, for example, permit doctors to refuse to participate in hastening patient deaths. Similarly, no doctor in the United States is forced to perform abortions. Indeed, when New York mayor Michael Bloomberg sought to increase accessibility to abortion by requiring that all residents in obstetrics and gynecology in New York's public hospitals receive training in pregnancy termination, the law specifically allowed doctors with religious or moral objections to opt out through a conscience clause.

This comity permits all who possess the requisite talent and intelligence to pursue medical careers without compromising their fundamental moral beliefs. But that may be about to change. Tolerance toward dissenters of what might be called the "new medicine" is quickly eroding. Courts, policymakers, media leaders—even the elites of organized medicine—increasingly assert that patient rights and respect for patients' choices should trump the consciences of medical professionals. Indeed, the time may soon arrive when doctors, nurses, and pharmacists will be compelled to take, or be complicit in the taking of, human life, regardless of their strong religious or moral objections thereto.

Coercing Doctors to Kill

A recent article published by bioethicist Jacob Appel provides a glimpse of the emerging rationale behind the coming coercion. As the Montana Supreme Court pondered whether to affirm a trial judge's ruling creating a state constitutional right to assisted suicide, Appel opined that justices should not only validate the "right to die" but also, in effect, establish a physician's duty to kill, predicated on the medical monopoly possessed by license practitioners. "Much as the government has been willing to impose duties on radio stations (e.g., indecency codes, equal-time rules) that would be impermissible if applied to newspapers," Appel wrote. "Montana might reasonably consider requiring physicians, in return for the privilege of a medical license, to prescribe medication to the dying without regard to the patient's intent." Should the court not thus guarantee access to assisted suicide, it would be merely creating "a theoretical right to die that cannot be meaningfully exercised."

Indeed, forcing medical professionals to participate in the taking of human life is already advancing into the justifiable stage. In Washington, a pharmacy chain refused to carry an abortifacient contraceptive that violated the religious views of its owners. A trial judge ruled that the owners were protected in making this decision by the First Amendment. But in *Stormans Inc. v. Selecky* [2009], the Ninth Circuit Court of Appeals reversed the decision, ruling that a state regulation that all legal prescriptions be filled was enforceable against the company because it was a law of general applicability and did not target religion.

In a decision that should chill the blood of everyone who believes in religious freedom, the court stated: "That the new rules prohibit all improper reasons for refusal to dispense medication ... suggests that the purpose of the new rules was not to eliminate religious objections to delivery of lawful medicines but to eliminate all objections that do not ensure patient health, safety, and access to medication. Thus, the rules do not target practices because of their religious motivation." And since pharmacists are not among the medical professionals allowed by Washington's law to refuse participation in assisted suicide, *Stormans* would also seem to compel dispensing lethal prescriptions for legally qualified patients even though the drugs are expressly intended to kill.

Unconscionable Acts

It isn't just the courts. Many of the most notable professional medical organizations are also hostile to protecting medical conscience rights. In 2007, for example, the American College of Obstetricians and Gynecologists (ACOG) published an ethics-committee opinion denying its members the right of conscience against abortion:

> Although respect for conscience is important, conscientious refusals should be limited if they constitute an imposition of religious and moral beliefs on patients. ... Physicians and other healthcare providers have the duty to refer patients in a timely manner to other providers if they do not feel they can in conscience provide the standard reproductive services that patients request. ... Providers with moral or religious objections should either practice in proximity to individuals who share their views or ensure that referral processes are in place. In an emergency in which referral is not possible or might negatively impact a patient's physical or mental health, providers have an obligation to provide medically indicated requested care.

If this view is ever mandated legally, every obstetrician and gynecologist in America will be required either to perform abortions or to be complicit in them by finding a willing doc-

State-Controlled Medicine

All Americans would do well to remember the tragic lessons of history in regard to regimes that force their medical doctors to kill in the name of the "common good," as defined by the state. Nazi Germany did not commit the first state-sanctioned genocide, but it was the first nation to medicalize the process. Social Darwinists and eugenics scientists made the decisions on who would live and who would die, according to their ideas about the utilitarian purpose of human life.

Kyle-Anne Shiver, American Thinker,
April 8, 2009. www.americanthinker.com

tor for the patient. And don't think that can't happen. A law enacted in Victoria, Australia (the Abortion Law Reform Act of 2008) imposes that very legal duty on every doctor. The law states:

> If a woman requests a registered health practitioner to advise on a proposed abortion, or to perform, direct, authorize, or supervise an abortion for that woman, and the practitioner has a conscientious objection to abortion, the practitioner must—(a) inform the woman that the practitioner has a conscientious objection to abortion; and (b) refer the woman to another registered health practitioner in the same regulated health profession who the practitioner knows does not have a conscientious objection to abortion.

Endorsing Euthanasia

Recent California legislation for what could be called euthanasia by the back door attempted to incorporate the same approach. As originally written, AB 2747 would have granted terminally ill patients—defined in the bill as persons having one year or less to live—the right to demand "palliative seda-tion" from their doctors. The bill was subversive on two fronts. First, it redefined a proper and ethical palliative technique, in which a patient who is near death, and whose suffering can-not otherwise be alleviated, is put into an artificial coma until natural death from the disease occurs. But as originally writ-ten, the bill redefined, as a method of killing, "the use of seda-tive medications to relieve extreme suffering by making the patient unaware and unconscious, while artificial food and hy-dration are withheld, during the progression of the disease, leading to the death of the patient." In other words, the bill sought to legalize active euthanasia via sedation and dehydra-tion.

Second, it would have granted patients with a year or less to live the right to be sedated and dehydrated *on demand*. And it wouldn't matter whether the physician didn't believe that the patient's symptoms warranted sedation or whether he or she objected morally to killing the patient: Physicians asked by qualified patients to be terminally sedated would have had the duty to comply or refer. (The bill ultimately passed without these objectionable provisions and without the improper defi-nition of palliative sedation.)

Here's another example of intolerance of medical con-science: In the waning days of the [George W.] Bush adminis-tration, the Department of Health and Human Services issued a rule preventing employment discrimination against medical professionals who refuse to perform a medical service because it violates their religious or moral beliefs. Based on the decibel level of the opposition, one would have thought that *Roe v. Wade* had been overturned. "That meddlesome regulation en-couraging healthcare workers to obstruct needed treatment considered offensive," Barbara Coombs Lee, the head of Com-passion and Choices, railed on her blog, "allows ideologues in health care to place their own dogmatic beliefs above all." Pro-tecting the consciences of dissenting medical professionals is "dangerous," she wrote, because "it's like a big doggy treat for healthcare bulldogs who would love to sink their teeth into other people's healthcare decisions."

It wasn't just overt true believers like Lee. Even before the final rule was published in the *Federal Register*, [U.S. senators] Hillary Clinton and Patty Murray introduced a bill to prevent the rule from going into effect. Immediately following its promulgation, Connecticut—joined by California, Illinois, Massachusetts, New Jersey, Oregon, and Rhode Island, and supported by the ACLU [American Civil Liberties Union]—filed suit to enjoin the regulation from being enforced. One of the [Barack] Obama administration's first public acts was to file in the *Federal Register* a notice of its intent to rescind the Bush conscience regulation.

Newspaper editorial pages throughout the nation exploded, opening another front against the rule. The *New York Times* called it an "awful regulation" and a "parting gift to the far right." The *St. Louis Post-Dispatch* went so far as to state: "Doctors, nurses, and pharmacists choose professions that put patients' rights first. If they foresee that priority becoming problematic for them, they should choose another profession." In other words, physicians and other medical professionals who want to adhere to the traditional Hippocratic ethic should be persona non grata in medicine—an astonishing assertion.

Binding Conscience Clauses

Society is approaching a crucial crossroads. It seems clear that the drive to include death-inducing techniques as legal and legitimate methods of medical care will only accelerate in the coming years. If doctors and other medical professionals are forced to participate in these new approaches or get out of health care, it will mark the end of the principles contained in the Hippocratic Oath as viable ethical protections for both patients and medical professionals.

True, healthcare workers enjoy some state and federal legal conscience protections. But a cold wind is blowing, threatening to end the current comity. If Hippocratic medicine is to be salvaged, the rights of medical conscience need to be expanded and made explicit. With the understanding that there may be nuances in specific circumstances not discussed here, I suggest that the following general principles apply in crafting such protections:

- Conscience clauses should be legally binding.

- The rights of conscience should apply to medical facilities such as hospitals and nursing homes as well as to individuals.

- Except in rare and compelling circumstances in which a patient's life is at stake, no medical professional should be compelled to perform or participate in procedures or treatments that take human life.

- The rights of conscience should apply most strongly in *elective procedures*, that is, medical treatments not required to extend the life of, or prevent serious harm to, the patient.

- It should be the *procedure* that is objectionable, not the patient. In this way, for example, physicians could not refuse to treat a lung-cancer patient because the patient smoked or to maintain the life of a patient in a vegetative state because the physician believed that people with profound impairments do not have a life worth living.

- No medical professional should ever be forced to participate in a medical procedure intended primarily to facilitate the patient's lifestyle preferences or desires (in contrast to maintaining life or treating a disease or injury).

- To avoid conflicts and respect patient autonomy, patients should be advised, whenever feasible, in advance of a professional's or facility's conscientious objection to performing or participating in legal medical procedures or treatments.

- The rights of conscience should be limited to bona fide medical facilities such as hospitals, skilled nursing centers, and hospices and to licensed medical professionals such as physicians, nurses, and pharmacists.

It is a sad day when medical professionals and facilities have to be protected legally from coerced participation in life-terminating medical procedures. But there is no denying the direction in which the scientific and moral currents are flowing. With ethical views in society and medicine growing increasingly polyglot [diverse], with the sanctity of human life increasingly under a cloud in the medical context, and given the establishment's marked hostility toward medical professionals who adhere to the traditional Hippocratic maxims, conscience clauses may be the only shelter protecting traditional morality in medicine.

> *"What [conscience clauses] would protect is not just the workers' tender consciences but also their right to not work and to not get disciplined for such refusals."*

Medical Practitioners Should Not Be Protected by Conscience Clauses

Jaana Goodrich

Jaana Goodrich is a former economist who now operates the political Web log Echidne of the Snakes. She insists in the viewpoint that follows that always protecting medical practitioners with conscience clauses is unreasonable. As Goodrich explains, pharmacists who refuse to dispense medicine that conflicts with their moral beliefs is tantamount to giving them the right to decide who can and cannot receive treatment. Shielding these pharmacists, she claims, is irrational because theoretically some could simply continue to withhold services while collecting a paycheck for doing nothing.

J. Goodrich, "The Conscience Clause," *American Prospect*, vol. 17, April 2006, p. 9. Copyright © 2006 The American Prospect, Inc. All rights reserved. Reproduced with permission from *The American Prospect*, 11 Beacon Street, Suite 1120, Boston, MA 02108.

As you read, consider the following questions:

1. How has the Christian right stolen the liberals' "toolkit," in Goodrich's view?

2. How does the author define discrimination in the legal sense?

3. What does Goodrich believe is the real motive behind conscience clauses?

We liberals have a lot on our consciences. Who taught the right wing how to use religion for social causes during the Martin Luther King era? Who showed them that discrimination on the basis of race or sex was not something most Americans see as part of the generous bounty of this country? It was us, and now we reap the harvest of all these past successes: The Christian right has stolen our toolkit and is busily using it to demolish the human rights we so laboriously built. They tell us that religious people are the real victims of discrimination and they tell us that what really oppresses them is—human rights. Who would have thought.

The human rights the Christian right deplores most are women's reproductive rights. These rights oppress pro-life pharmacists all across the country, pharmacists who have decided to believe that the contraceptive pill, including its stronger "Morning After" or Plan B form, amounts to the killing of unborn babies. These pharmacists have no desire to fill such prescriptions that would do that, even if the prescription is for the treatment of some malady quite unrelated to birth control.

Lucky for them, someone is looking out for their rights: Legislators in several states have proposed bills that would protect the rights of a pro-life pharmacist—even one wishing to deny a customer her emergency contraceptive pills late at night in some solitary rural pharmacy when there are no other routes to obtain them—by instituting lefty-sounding

"Health Care Workers' Rights" or "Pharmacist Conscience Clauses." What these laws would protect is not just the workers' tender consciences but also their right to not work and to not get disciplined for such refusals. We should all be so lucky.

Take the bill proposed for the protection of pro-life pharmacists in the state of Missouri. Among other goodies, it promises that pharmacists will be protected against discrimination: "Employers cannot refuse to hire, discriminate against, segregate, or terminate a pharmaceutical professional because of their opposition to any service involving a particular drug or device that they have a good faith belief is used for abortions."

See what I mean about the right having stolen our toolkit? They have taken "discrimination," and they are using it all wrong. If I refuse to hire a pharmacist just because that person is black or female or a Unitarian, I am discriminating in the legal sense because all these characteristics are irrelevant from the point of view of what pharmacists are expected to do. What is not irrelevant is whether the pharmacist will actually do the job I'm trying to fill, and yet this is exactly what the right-wing Christians are arguing. "Discrimination" has had the usual fate of terms stolen by the right wing: Its meaning has been turned on its head.

The Missouri bill doesn't just privilege the consciences of pharmacists over the still legally protected reproductive rights of women. Although it is careful to limit the conscience clause to qualms about abortion, the problem it reflects is more general: The ethical values of a worker are given priority, even when these values interfere with the perfectly legal job the worker has been hired for and even when the refusal to dispense a medication may result in serious harm to the patients the pharmacy is paid to serve. Christian Scientists don't believe in conventional medical care. Could a Christian Scientist work as a pharmacist somewhere in this country, spending

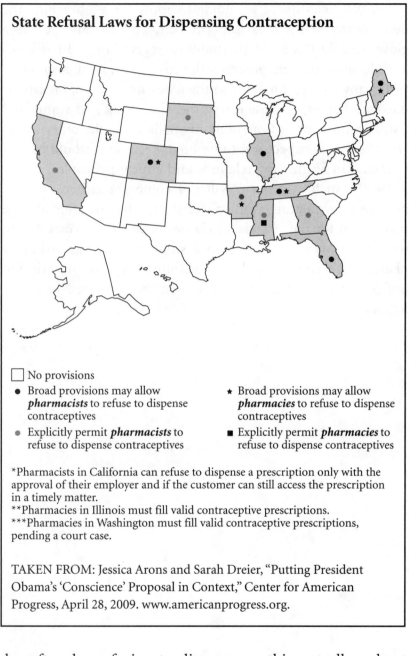

State Refusal Laws for Dispensing Contraception

☐ No provisions

● Broad provisions may allow *pharmacists* to refuse to dispense contraceptives

● Explicitly permit *pharmacists* to refuse to dispense contraceptives

★ Broad provisions may allow *pharmacies* to refuse to dispense contraceptives

■ Explicitly permit *pharmacies* to refuse to dispense contraceptives

*Pharmacists in California can refuse to dispense a prescription only with the approval of their employer and if the customer can still access the prescription in a timely matter.
**Pharmacies in Illinois must fill valid contraceptive prescriptions.
***Pharmacies in Washington must fill valid contraceptive prescriptions, pending a court case.

TAKEN FROM: Jessica Arons and Sarah Dreier, "Putting President Obama's 'Conscience' Proposal in Context," Center for American Progress, April 28, 2009. www.americanprogress.org.

day after day refusing to dispense anything at all, and yet cashing in a salary every month? It is beginning to look like a real possibility.

In the meantime, I am going to apply for a job behind the deli counter at my local supermarket. The job fits me like a glove because I'm a fanatic Buddhist vegetarian and I will enjoy educating and enlightening the customers. I will also refuse to fill any orders for ham sandwiches or chicken breasts or meatball heroes, because eating meat is wrong and sinful, and I will spend a lot of time filing my nails while the other workers take over. I expect not to be fired, because it would be discrimination against my religious and ethical principles.

Sadly, such a scenario will not come about because it is not about regulating women's fertility. That is, after all, the real reason for the conscience clauses: The Uterus Wars. If you wish to convince me otherwise show me the case where a pharmacist's conscience left a customer's Viagra prescription unfilled or the packet of condoms on the counter. Not gonna happen.

> *"Pastors spoke freely about the policy positions of candidates for elective office throughout American history, even endorsing or opposing candidates from the pulpit."*

Preachers Should Be Allowed to Endorse Political Candidates from the Pulpit

Ron Johnson Jr.

Ron Johnson Jr. is the senior associate pastor of the Living Stones Fellowship Church in Crown Point, Indiana. He asserts in the following viewpoint that churches and their pastors should not be silenced on political topics just because the Internal Revenue Service mandated in 1954 that the tax exemption afforded to churches requires them to refrain from endorsing political candidates. Johnson points out that, before the 1954 law, church leaders enjoyed the right to endorse candidates and speak freely on any number of political topics. This, he says, is the right afforded to all Americans under the First Amendment. Johnson believes

Ron Johnson Jr., "IRS Should Not Keep Churches out of Politics," *U.S. News & World Report*, November 10, 2008. Copyright © 2008 U.S. News & World Report, L.P. All rights reserved. Reprinted with permission.

that pastors have the right to address their congregations on any topic that is relevant to the church community without jeopardizing their tax-exempt status.

As you read, consider the following questions:

1. According to Johnson, what is the purpose of the Pulpit Initiative?

2. What does the author say the IRS failed to do in 1954 when it passed its tax code stipulation that forbade pastors to endorse political candidates?

3. Why does Johnson believe the church unquestioningly deserves its tax exempt status?

Who is in charge of the pulpit? The church or the IRS? That is the question that recently led me and other pastors to deliver sermons on the subject of the upcoming elections, despite tax rules used to stifle speech about candidates. The sermons were part of a broader effort, the Alliance Defense Fund's Pulpit Initiative, which is designed to protect pastors' First Amendment rights.

I wish to be clear from the outset. I have no desire to turn my pulpit into a Christian version of the Chicago political machine. My church will not be writing large checks to candidates, or to anyone else for that matter. We have plenty to do educating Christians about tithing to support the church, let alone political campaigns.

I have no intention of selecting my sermon topics by watching CNN or Fox News. I have no secret dream of becoming president or even running for dogcatcher. To suggest, as some have, that somehow we are being seduced by political power or that we are looking to government to be America's "savior" is silliness. And no, the Pulpit Initiative is not about encouraging pastors to endorse candidates from the pulpit.

Right to Tax Exemption

The state cannot demand the surrender of constitutional rights for a church to remain tax exempt. Nonprofit organizations are exempted because they are not profit-makers. If citizens are already taxed on their individual incomes, taxing their participation in a voluntary organization from which they derive no monetary gain amounts to double taxation.

Churches are all the more tax exempt. Church tax exemption is not a gift, nor is it a "subsidy," as some disingenuously contend.

Erik Stanley,
Townhall.com, September 8, 2008.

Restoring the Right to Free Speech

The purpose of the Pulpit Initiative is to restore the right of pastors to speak freely from the pulpit without fear of punishment by the government for doing what churches do: speak on any number of cultural and societal issues from a biblical perspective. Christians believe that civil government owes its existence to God and is therefore accountable to him to behave righteously in serving the common good. A significant role of the church is—and always has been—to encourage the civil magistrate to do what is good and not what is evil.

The Internal Revenue Service has placed itself in the role of evaluating the content of a pastor's sermon to determine if the message is "political." We need to ask: Where did this authority come from? And why should Americans be willing to submit to this unconstitutional power grab without even a whimper? Why are pastors the only people who have allowed the IRS to censor their First Amendment rights for a tax exemption they have enjoyed since the founding of our nation—a tax exemption that existed long before the IRS did?

A False Dichotomy

Erik Stanley, the head of the Pulpit Initiative, has rightly pointed out that pastors spoke freely about the policy positions of candidates for elective office throughout American history, even endorsing or opposing candidates from the pulpit, without anyone ever questioning whether churches should remain tax exempt. It was commonplace—even expected—for pastors to speak in support of or in opposition to candidates until the tax code was amended in 1954 with no legislative analysis or debate.

Churches are tax exempt because they are churches, not because the government decided to bless them with a "subsidy." The church is not a profit-making business or individual. It is not getting a pass on taxes; it is simply outside the government's appropriate tax base.

Secularists often create a false sacred/secular dichotomy that conveniently silences our message. While it's true that pastors need to stop letting others tell us to keep Jesus inside of the church and out of the world he died to redeem, this particular battle is about whether we as pastors even have the right to speak as we feel led to within our own four walls.

A Pastor's Choice

The Pulpit Initiative is not about promoting political parties or agendas or establishing a "theocracy." It's about our right to bring kingdom principles and solutions to bear on contemporary social problems if we so choose. A pastor may choose not to, but it's the pastor's choice, not the choice of the IRS.

If we cannot discuss any and all topics, including those the IRS may deem "political," even within our communities of faith, we will become what Martin Luther King Jr. called an "irrelevant social club without moral or spiritual authority."

Simply put, it's time for the church to be the church.

> "[Preachers] must not endorse particu-
> lar candidates, raise money for their
> campaigns or parties or offer favors not
> extended to others."

Preachers Should Not Be Allowed to Endorse Political Candidates from the Pulpit

Eric Williams

In the following viewpoint, Eric Williams argues that clergy should not endorse candidates from the pulpit. In Williams's opinion, preachers should respect the political diversity of their congregations and refrain from using their position of authority to influence voters. Williams states that the purpose of religion is to bring communal and individual change on a spiritual level and not to engage in political debate. Eric Williams is senior pastor of North Congregational United Church of Christ in Columbus, Ohio.

As you read, consider the following questions:

1. How does Williams define the functions of the wall that separates church and state?

Eric Williams, "Should Clergy Use Pulpit to Endorse Candidates? No," *Columbus Dispatch*, September 22, 2008. Copyright © 2008, The Columbus Dispatch. Reproduced by permission.

2. What does the author believe is the true motive for the Alliance Defense Fund's Pulpit Initiative?

3. According to Williams, what is the only way in which clergy members should endorse or oppose political candidates?

On May 5, [2008] the Alliance Defense Fund [ADR] sent a letter encouraging me to commit tax abuse in the pulpit this Sunday by preaching a sermon "specifically opposing candidates for office whose political positions conflict with Scriptural truth."

The ADF is attempting to tear down the wall that separates church and state. This wall protects citizens from the hurricanes of religious extremism; it is the fencerow that encourages us to be caring neighbors; it is the mile marker erected by the Founders to guide faithful patriots in each new generation, who seek and secure for everyone our unalienable rights of "life, liberty and the pursuit of happiness."

It is the hope of the ADF that clergy in many states and from many traditions will participate in what it calls the Pulpit Initiative. It is my hope that none will consent. The vitality of America's faith community and the strength of its life-affirming witness are found in its respect for our nation's religious diversity, as well as its commitment to champion and serve society's most pressing concerns.

Respecting Diversity

Just as the people have many perspectives on faith and Scriptural truth, we are equally diverse when it comes to electoral politics. We are Republicans, Democrats and independents. We are liberals, conservatives and moderates. As leaders of communities of faith, it is important to engage the important moral and political issues of the day. Our national commitment to diversity and justice for all binds us together across our convictions, creeds and practices.

To fulfill the role of the faith community in society, it is necessary to understand the difference between political and electoral activity. We need to know the church-state line and we need to step up to it—but we must avoid crossing it. As leaders and communities of faith, we are called to be God's prophetic and pastoral voices. We can raise difficult issues. We can hold challenging forums. We can champion important causes but we must not endorse particular candidates, raise money for their campaigns or parties or offer favors not extended to others.

The role of religion in our society—to bring lasting and transforming change, both personally and communally—is always greater than any single candidate, party or election. For leaders and communities of faith to lose perspective of God's long-term reign of peace with justice by focusing on a single candidate is not only illegal but also shortsighted.

As registered voters, the electoral process belongs to each one of us. As leaders and communities of faith, however, we fulfill our role in society by being merciful, speaking truth to power, educating our members and neighbors about important issues, encouraging all to vote their convictions, praying for our public servants and honoring the separation of religion and state.

Free Speech Not the Issue

The ADF wants us to believe that its Pulpit Initiative is a call to restore freedom of speech to the pulpit. Free speech is not in question; it is the use of tax-exempt dollars for electoral politics that is prohibited. More, telling participants of the worship community whom to vote for violates each listener's freedom of choice. Please don't abuse the power of the pulpit. Instead, inspire and equip listeners to understand pressing moral and political issues so that each confidently will vote the convictions of their own conscience. Don't seek to impose

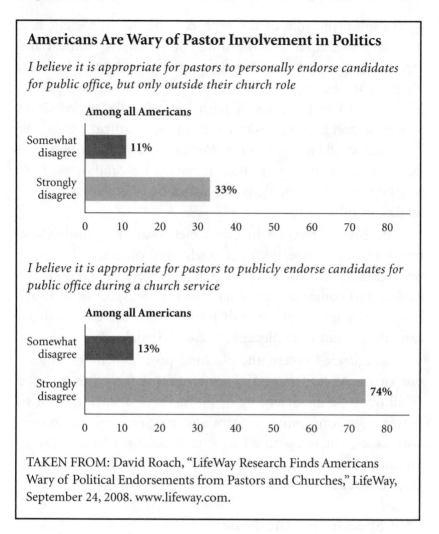

Americans Are Wary of Pastor Involvement in Politics

I believe it is appropriate for pastors to personally endorse candidates for public office, but only outside their church role

Among all Americans

Somewhat disagree — 11%

Strongly disagree — 33%

0 10 20 30 40 50 60 70 80

I believe it is appropriate for pastors to publicly endorse candidates for public office during a church service

Among all Americans

Somewhat disagree — 13%

Strongly disagree — 74%

0 10 20 30 40 50 60 70 80

TAKEN FROM: David Roach, "LifeWay Research Finds Americans Wary of Political Endorsements from Pastors and Churches," LifeWay, September 24, 2008. www.lifeway.com.

religious values on your neighbors, but value the collective wisdom of community dialogue, where all voices are respected and welcome.

If any of my colleagues in the clergy seek to oppose a candidate, I ask that they do so as private citizens. If any desire to endorse a candidate from the pulpit, I remind them that they jeopardize their faith community's tax-exempt status and compromise their religious authority by aligning with political power. If seeking influence over government policy and practice is their goal, I advise them to do so as campaign organizers or lobbyists.

I share a recently expressed view that tax-exempt charitable organizations are given a tax break because they do good works that transcend politics.

As the leader of a faith community, I respect that some of my colleagues might feel compelled to protest a law they think unjust or inconsistent with their religious beliefs, and I appreciate that the First Amendment protects that sort of expression. However, the Pulpit Initiative is not a mere protest; it is as if a group of lawyers have stepped into the pulpit to coordinate a mass violation of federal law. Even if ADF's intentions are understandable, I cannot condone this inappropriate, unethical and illegal behavior.

Periodical Bibliography

The following articles have been selected to supplement the diverse views presented in this chapter.

Sandhya Bathija	"Whose Conscience Counts?" *Church & State*, October 2009.
Rob Boston	"Faith and Freedom: What's Conservative About School Prayer," *Humanist*, May–June 2009.
Christianity Today	"Oversight Overstep," January 2008.
John M. D'Arcy	"The Church and the University," *America*, August 31, 2009.
Ross Douthat	"Let's Talk About Faith," *New York Times*, January 11, 2010.
Martha McCarthy	"Beyond the Wall of Separation: Church-State Concerns in Public Schools," *Phi Delta Kappan*, June 2009.
Stephen Prothero	"Worshiping in Ignorance," *Chronicle of Higher Education*, March 16, 2007.
Dolores T. Puterbaugh	"Freedom Foregone," *USA Today* (magazine), March 2009.
Brad Rothrock	"God and the Teenage Mind," *America*, September 14, 2009.
Janet E. Smith	"Conscience and Uncontroversial Truths," *Priest*, January 2009.

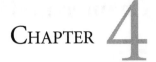

CHAPTER 4

What Values Should Religious Americans Support?

Chapter Preface

During the 2008 presidential election, Christians in the United States were divided on their opinions of the Democratic frontrunner, Senator Barack Obama. Many Christians had supported the conservative values embodied in the presidency of George W. Bush, but not all saw his potential Republican successor, John McCain, as a worthy, religious-minded candidate. McCain shied away from discussions of religion, and his own faith was the subject of some controversy. Obama, on the other hand, had to lay bare his religious convictions during the presidential race. Fighting off accusations that he was a Muslim (which some equate with having terrorist sympathies), Obama asserted that he belonged to the Trinity United Church of Christ in Chicago and that faith played a very important role in his life. "My faith informs my values, and in that sense it helps shape my worldview, and I don't think anyone should be required to leave their religious sensibilities at the door," he told the *Concord Monitor*, a New Hampshire newspaper, during the presidential race.

Despite his statements, many Christians were suspicious of Obama because he professed traditionally liberal views about such polarizing issues as abortion and gay rights. Robert A.J. Gagnon, an associate professor at the Pittsburgh Theological Seminary, wrote an angry broadside in November 2008 in which he insisted "the country's legal and moral stance on abortion and especially homosexual practice will deteriorate rapidly and likely remain in a deteriorated state for at least decades to come" if Barack Obama won the presidency. Gagnon and others like him argued that these two fundamental issues could not be compromised by the Christian community. Joe Green, an associate minister in Pennsylvania, feared that the election of Obama would mean that deeply held religious views would simply be ignored in America. "I sincerely believe that we are about to face some very trying times in the near future," Green wrote on the Josiah Generation Ministries Web site. "As a Christian living by the standards of the Word of God, we will be facing a serious, uphill battle, and if we do not stand up for Christian values, we will be silenced forever."

Not all American Christians, however, voted according to the candidates' stances on abortion and issues relating to homosexuality. Nearly half of those who define themselves as born-again Christians supported Obama in the election because of his economic policies and his position on the war in Iraq. Dave Kinnaman, president of The Barna Group, a research organization that examines the intersection of faith and culture, acknowledged, "The Christian community . . . is more open to this Democratic candidate than we've been in at least the last couple national elections." Some rightly noted that conservative presidents failed to dismantle *Roe v. Wade*, and thus they did not believe the issue of abortion law was meant to be the deciding factor when casting their vote for a Democratic leader. Others—especially moderate Christians—argued that Obama's presidency promised a change on many issues and a chance to reshape America's global reputation, which many contend was neglected or even tarnished under the George W. Bush administration.

In the following chapter, the authors examine issues such as abortion and same-sex marriage and suggest how religious Americans should position themselves in regard to these matters. Some advocate a strict separation between politics and faith, while others believe that personal morality and the morality of the state should be the same in a country that professes itself to be "one nation under God."

| "Gay marriage is simply a bad idea,
| whether one is religious or not."

Christians Should Oppose Same-Sex Marriage

Mark Galli

Mark Galli is the senior managing editor of Christianity Today *and the author of* A Great and Terrible Love: A Spiritual Journey into the Attributes of God. *In the viewpoint that follows, Galli argues that gay marriage is one of many consequences of a culture that has embraced radical individualism over the larger, communal ideals of spiritual purpose and truth. In Galli's opinion, Christians as well as secular people have bought into the notion that personal interests and pleasures (bound up in the concept of individual rights) are paramount. He encourages Christians to reconsider this position and actively fight for scriptural values before the world descends further into darkness. Galli prompts believers to continue to oppose gay marriage as antithetical to biblical revelation.*

As you read, consider the following questions:

1. What was the first state court to rule that bans on gay marriage were unconstitutional, as Galli reports?

Mark Galli, "Is the Gay Marriage Debate Over?" *Christianity Today*, vol. 53, July 2009, pp. 30–33. Reproduced by permission of the author.

2. According to David Blankenhorn, as cited by Galli, what is the purpose of marriage?

3. How does the divorce rate among Christians undermine the fight against gay marriage, as explained by the author?

O ne could become wistful about the time in history when marriage was a settled affair, when everyone agreed on what it was, when no nation on the planet would have entertained the idea of legalizing same-sex marriage. But wistfulness is usually reserved for times long ago and places far away—not for a state of affairs that existed less than a decade ago.

In December 2000, the Dutch parliament became the first to pass legislation that gave same-sex couples the right to marry, divorce, and adopt children. On April 1 of the following year, the mayor of Amsterdam officiated, for the first time in human history, at the ceremonies of the first four gay couples. In the ensuing eight years, Belgium (2003), Spain (2005), Canada (2005), South Africa (2006), and Norway (2008) followed the Netherlands' lead, and Sweden may now not be far behind.

The U.S. Debate

While we shake our heads at those libertine Dutch, traditional marriage was challenged in the U.S. even earlier, in 1993, when the Hawaii Supreme Court ruled that the state's prohibition of same-sex marriages amounted to discrimination on the basis of sex. For the first time in U.S. history, a state supreme-court ruling suggested that gay couples may have the right to marry.

Social conservatives were galvanized into action and enacted a series of protective measures. Congress passed and President Bill Clinton signed the Defense of Marriage Act (doma) in 1996. Three states soon adopted constitutional same-sex marriage bans: Alaska (1998), Nebraska (2000), and Nevada (2000). And in a few years, 42 states enacted statutes similar to doma (although three of those bans have since been overturned).

Gay marriage advocacy was given new life with Massachusetts's historic 2003 high court ruling, which said that it was unconstitutional to deny same-sex couples the right to marry. It became clear that statutory bans were not enough; judges could throw out the laws if they felt the bans violated state constitutional rights. Over the next three years, voters in 23 states immediately amended their constitutions to limit marriage to heterosexuals.

Since then, the issue has ebbed and flowed, like trench warfare, with each side gaining only yards of territory with each new legislative or judicial assault. When the battle of Election 2008 had ended, it appeared that social conservatives had the momentum when constitutional amendments banning gay marriages passed in three more states.

Victories for the Opposition

But seemingly out of nowhere, gay marriage advocates have won stunning judicial, legislative, and social victories. Connecticut began granting marriage certificates to spouses of the same gender in November 2008. In April 2009, Iowa's high court ruled that banning gay marriages was unconstitutional, and gay couples began lining up at Iowa court houses. The Vermont legislature legalized gay marriage that same month, while Maine and New Hampshire legalized gay marriage in May.

All the while, [evangelical Christian minister] Rick Warren and Miss USA contestant Carrie Prejean were hit hard for their public statements against gay marriage. To be against gay marriage now carries a social stigma. A recent poll of Massachusetts residents revealed that 36 percent of voters who oppose gay marriage agreed with the statement, "If you speak

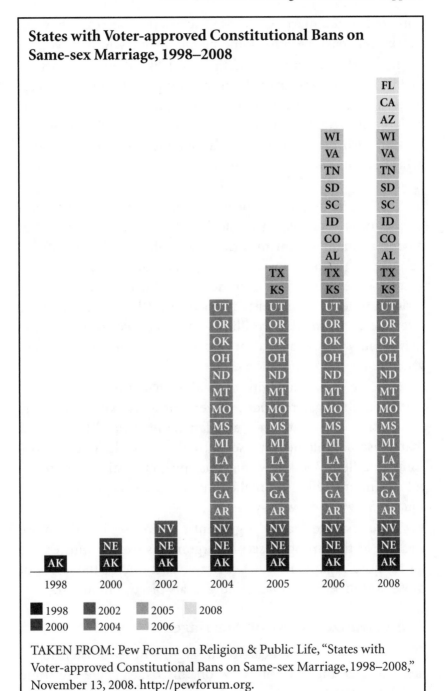

States with Voter-approved Constitutional Bans on Same-sex Marriage, 1998–2008

						FL
						CA
						AZ
					WI	WI
					VA	VA
					TN	TN
					SD	SD
					SC	SC
					ID	ID
					CO	CO
					AL	AL
				TX	TX	TX
				KS	KS	KS
			UT	UT	UT	UT
			OR	OR	OR	OR
			OK	OK	OK	OK
			OH	OH	OH	OH
			ND	ND	ND	ND
			MT	MT	MT	MT
			MO	MO	MO	MO
			MS	MS	MS	MS
			MI	MI	MI	MI
			LA	LA	LA	LA
			KY	KY	KY	KY
			GA	GA	GA	GA
			AR	AR	AR	AR
		NV	NV	NV	NV	NV
	NE	NE	NE	NE	NE	NE
AK	AK	AK	AK	AK	AK	AK
1998	2000	2002	2004	2005	2006	2008

■ 1998   ■ 2002   ■ 2005   ■ 2008
■ 2000   ■ 2004   ■ 2006

TAKEN FROM: Pew Forum on Religion & Public Life, "States with Voter-approved Constitutional Bans on Same-sex Marriage, 1998–2008," November 13, 2008. http://pewforum.org.

out against gay marriage in Massachusetts you really have to watch your back because some people may try to hurt you."

In short, traditional Christians feel like the armored tank of history is rolling over them, crushing traditional marriage under its iron treads, impervious to argument, the ballot box, or judicial logic. Even more disheartening has been to witness how, in each mainline denomination, and even in some evangelical seminaries, fellow Christians lobby hard for gay marriage.

The depressing feeling of inevitability is precisely what advocates of gay marriage want to instill in their opponents. But relying as many do on historical determinism—"Side with us because we're going to win"—suggests that gay marriage advocates have run out of arguments. It also demonstrates historical amnesia. Arguments from historical inevitability have often been assumed by millions—to take two examples, the inevitability of Communism and the death of religion—and yet have proven to be wrong.

Still, we are at our wits' ends about what to say next, impervious as the gay marriage juggernaut is. We know biblically and instinctively that "male and female he created them," and that these complementary sexual beings are designed to become one flesh. We know that this spiritual instinct and biblical argument will not make much headway in the public square. So what do we say?

We can make secular arguments, of course, but the more we look at the strongest secular arguments we can muster, the more those arguments cut two ways. And one of the edges of those arguments will make evangelicals bleed, I'm afraid.

The Privatized View of Marriage

One way to get at the heart of an argument is to listen to allies who take the opposite view on this issue. There are some social conservatives, for example, who argue for gay marriage on conservative grounds.

Take *The Atlantic's* foremost blogger, Andrew Sullivan, a Roman Catholic. He also happens to be gay, but his argument does not rest on his sexual preference. His case, as he asserted in a *2003 Time essay*, is "an eminently conservative one—in fact, almost an emblem of 'compassionate conservatism.'" He says the institution of marriage fosters responsibility, commitment, and the domestication of unruly men. Thus, "bringing gay men and women into this institution will surely change the gay subculture in subtle but profoundly conservative ways." Growing up gay, he realized he would never have a family, and that it's "the weddings and relationships and holidays that give families structure and meaning." And thus, "when I looked forward, I saw nothing but emptiness and loneliness. No wonder it was hard to connect sex with love and commitment," Sullivan wrote.

Or take the argument from the street, so to speak, from a common blogger in Algonquin, Illinois. He is a heterosexual who lives with a woman, and a political conservative who supports legalizing gay marriage. He says we must accept the fact that American society has moved on and "embraced different ways people choose to live and love." And "when you take away all the legalisms, the moral quotient, the religious implications, and the needs of society," he writes, "what we are left with is nothing more than how people choose to define their relationships where they feel love for another human being."

These two writers—one from the center of American culture and the other from the heartland—summarize a privatized view of marriage. Marriage is about the fulfillment of the two people involved. It will help them to mature as human beings and to express more deeply their love for one another.

Marriage Is About Reproduction

This, of course, strikes at the heart of how Christians have traditionally understood marriage. David Blankenhorn, president of the New York–based Institute for American Values and author of *The Future of Marriage*, argued this in a nonreligious way in a September 2008 *Los Angeles Times* op-ed. There is one constant in the constantly evolving understanding of marriage, he says: "In all societies, marriage shapes the rights and obligations of parenthood. Among us humans, the scholars report, marriage is not primarily a license to have sex. Nor is it primarily a license to receive benefits or social recognition. It is primarily a license to have children."

Further, he says, "Marriage says to a child: The man and the woman whose sexual union made you will also be there to love and raise you. Marriage says to society as a whole: For every child born, there is a recognized mother and a father, accountable to the child and to each other."

The argument is nuanced, and goes on to take into account heterosexual couples who will not or cannot have children. But he grounds marriage not in two people, but in two communities: the family and the state.

McGill University law professor Margaret Somerville, in a 2003 brief before Canada's Standing Committee on Justice and Human Rights, argued in much the same way. She says that to form a society, we must create "a societal-cultural paradigm." This is a constellation of "values, principles, attitudes, beliefs, and myths" by which a society finds value and meaning, both individually and collectively.

"Reproduction is the fundamental occurrence on which, ultimately, the future of human life depends," she says. "That is the primary reason why marriage is important to society." Thus, it is crucial that societies protect marriage as a fact and as a symbol, as that institution that fosters human life, doing so in the context of family and society. "Even if a particular man and woman cannot or do not want to have a child, their getting married does not damage this general symbolism."

Again, the argument is involved and nuanced. Both Blankenhorn and Somerville ground marriage in something larger than two selves who wish to find fulfillment. Marriage is inescapably connected to children and thus family, and family is inescapably connected to society.

In a highly individualistic culture, this argument swims upstream, but conservative Christians recognize that it corresponds to their basic theological instincts. The narcissism of mutual self-fulfillment will never be a solid foundation for a particular marriage, let alone for the most fundamental institution in society. This is an argument we can press publicly as the opportunity arises.

We'll have to press it humbly, however, because as it turns out, we are very much complicit in the unrighteousness we decry.

A Nation of Hypocrites

The thrust of the pro–gay-marriage argument rests on the assumption that the happiness of the individual is paramount, and that the state's responsibility is to protect the rights of individuals to pursue whatever they think will make them happy, as long as no one gets hurt. The irony of radical individualism is that it will eventually hurt somebody. In practice, the happiness of one individual always runs into the happiness of another, and then only the strong survive. The weaker individual is no longer treated as fully human, and thus his or her right to happiness is compromised. In our nation, we see this in the way we treat individuals at both ends of life, in how expendable they are if they interrupt the happiness of the fully functioning—take the increasing acceptance of euthanasia, and the on-the-ground fact of abortions in the thousands every day.

Evangelicals are sensitive to this reality, but are less aware of how much we proactively participate in the culture of individualism. While stopping short of abortion, we have not given much thought to our easy acceptance of artificial contraception. I'm not arguing for or against contraception here, only pointing to the reality that contraception has separated sex from procreation. That, in turn, has prompted most couples, evangelicals included, to think that sex is first and foremost a fulfilling psychological and physical experience, that a couple has a right to enjoy themselves for a few years before they settle down to family life.

In essence, we have already redefined marriage as an institution designed for personal happiness. We see ancillary evidence of this at the other end of marriage: Though it is a difficult thing to measure, the rate at which evangelicals divorce is hard to distinguish from the larger culture's, and the list of reasons for divorce seems no different: "We grew apart." "We no longer met each other's needs." "Irreconcilable differences." The language of divorce is usually about the lack of self-fulfillment.

Add to that our penchant for changing churches, usually because "I just wasn't being fed," as well as our need to test every church and pastor against our personal reading of the Bible—well, you can see why Protestants have managed in 500 years to create out of two traditions (Orthodox and Catholic) some 30,000 denominations. While the Baptists are known for their doctrine of "soul competency," aversion of the doctrine is woven into the fabric of broader evangelicalism, though it has morphed into *sole* competency. Thus, the death of mutual accountability and church discipline in our movement. Thus, the exaltation of worship in which the personal experience of the worshiper so often becomes more important than the object of worship. Thus, the continual proliferation of churches, parachurches, and movements because the group we belong to just doesn't do it the way we think "the Lord is leading *me*" to do it.

We are, of all Christian traditions, the most individualistic. This individual emphasis has flourished in different ways and in different settings, and often for the good. It has challenged moribund religion (Reformation), prompted revival (Great Awakenings), ministered to the urban poor (Salvation Army), abolished slavery (William Wilberforce), and led to explosive worldwide church growth (Pentecostalism). But it is individualism nonetheless, and it cuts right to the heart of one of our best arguments against gay marriage.

We cannot very well argue for the sanctity of marriage as a crucial social institution while we blithely go about divorcing and approving of remarriage at a rate that destabilizes marriage. We cannot say that an institution, like the state, has a perfect right to insist on certain values and behavior from its citizens while we refuse to submit to denominational or local church authority. We cannot tell gay couples that marriage is about something much larger than self-fulfillment when we, like the rest of heterosexual culture, delay marriage until we can experience life, and delay having children until we can enjoy each other for a few years.

In short, we have been perfect hypocrites on this issue. Until we admit that, and take steps to mend our ways, our cries of alarm about gay marriage will echo off into oblivion.

The Fight Must Go On

This does not mean we should stop fighting initiatives that would legalize gay marriage. Gay marriage is simply a bad idea, whether one is religious or not. But it's bad not only because of what it *will* do to the social fabric, but because of what it signals *has already happened* to our social fabric. We are a culture of radical individualists, and gay marriage does nothing but put an exclamation point on that fact. We should fight it, because it will only make a bad situation worse.

That being said, we are as compromised as the next gay couple when it comes to radical individualism. This means that alongside our call to maintain traditional marriage, we should "bewail our manifold sins and wickedness," as the Book of Common Prayer puts it. We should acknowledge how much Protestant culture has shaped American culture, how much we've collaborated in the flowering of individualism, and how we continue to do so even when the flower has become a weed that is choking off life.

We well may lose the marriage war. But we are called into the battle not because we are promised victory, but because we're called to be witnesses of a greater battle. [Russian author] Aleksandr Solzhenitsyn has famously said that "the line separating good and evil passes not through states, nor between classes, nor between political parties either, but right through every human heart, and through all human hearts." In our time and place, it is a battle with the original temptation: to imagine we are gods, captains of our own souls and masters of our fate—a habitual unwillingness to submit to anything bigger than the self.

As we contend with gay marriage proponents, then, we contend as both prophets and penitents. Like Isaiah, we can announce to our culture the poisonous fruit of immorality, while saying, "Woe is me! For I am lost; for I am a man of unclean lips, and I dwell in the midst of a people of unclean lips." Like Paul, we can forthrightly warn others of the horrific consequences of sin, but in the next breath acknowledge that we must admit we are "the chief of sinners."

What we bring to the public table, then, is not our righteousness or even our humility. We come in the name of the One who came into the world to save sinners of all political and social persuasions. We raise our voices on behalf of righteousness not in a way calculated to win the culture—for sometimes we will, sometimes we won't—but as witnesses to the only Righteous One. We live in a culture that by all accounts is descending into darkness, and our job is to reflect the light of Christ. We speak for what *he* says is right, using the *lingua franca* of the culture to argue that as best we can, using the political and social instruments at our disposal to the best of our ability, acknowledging our own complicity in the sins we decry, and pointing to the One who must save us all.

> *"Should gay people be married in the same, sacramental sense that straight people are? I would argue that they should."*

Christians Should Support Same-Sex Marriage

Part I: John Bryson Chane; Part II: Lisa Miller

Though opponents of same-sex marriage often rely on Christian scripture to support their objections, many gay marriage advocates also utilize biblical passages and the teachings of Jesus to persuade audiences of the acceptability of these unions. In part I of the following viewpoint, John Bryson Chane, the Episcopal bishop of Washington, D.C., explains that marriage has evolved under church authority over the centuries to include a more equitable joining of man and wife. He believes that marriage can still evolve under Christian law to include same-sex couples because the loving commitment between two individuals is a reflection of God's love. In part II of this viewpoint, Lisa Miller carries Chane's argument further, claiming that much of biblical tradition has been obviated by modern realities. In her view, Christians often accept that many codified practices are out-

Part I: John Bryson Chane, "A Christian Case for Same-Sex Marriage," *Washington Post*, November 16, 2009. Reproduced by permission of the author. Part II: Lisa Miller, "Our Mutual Joy," *Newsweek*, vol. 152, December 15, 2008, pp. 28–31. Copyright © 2008 Newsweek, Inc. All rights reserved. Reproduced by permission.

dated, but the marriage between same-sex partners remains a sticking point. Miller points out that the Bible is full of nonconventional marriages and relationships and that the main message of the Scripture is inclusiveness. In her view, Christians who wish to conform to the teachings of the Bible should welcome more relations based on commitment and love.

As you read, consider the following questions:

1. According to Chane, when did the church acknowledge that the "mutual affection and self-sacrifice" elements of the marriage contract were of significant importance?

2. Why does Miller believe that the story of Adam and Eve is not a clear-cut example of marriage being restricted to the partnering of one man and one woman?

3. Why does Miller question the seriousness with which people treat the condemnation of homosexuality in the Bible?

Most media coverage of the [Washington] D.C. Council's steps toward civil marriage equality for same-sex couples [approved in 2009] has followed a worn-out script that gives the role of speaking for God to clergy who are opposed to equality. As the bishop of the Episcopal Diocese of Washington, I would say respectfully to my fellow Christians that people who deny others the blessings they claim for themselves should not assume they speak for the Almighty. And to journalists I would offer a short history of changing Christian understandings of the institution of marriage.

Christians have always argued about marriage. Jesus criticized the Mosaic law on divorce, saying "What God has joined together let no man separate." But we don't see clergy demanding that the city council make divorce illegal.

A History of Marriage and the Church

Some conservative Christian leaders claim that their understanding of marriage is central to Christian teaching. How do they square that claim with the Apostle Paul's teaching that marriage is an inferior state, one reserved for people who are not able to stay singly celibate and resist the temptation to fornication?

As historian Stephanie Coontz points out, the church did not bless marriages until the third century, or define marriage as a sacrament until 1215. The church embraced many of the assumptions of the patriarchal culture, in which women and marriageable children were assets to be controlled and exploited to the advantage of the man who headed their household. The theology of marriage was heavily influenced by economic and legal considerations; it emphasized procreation, and spoke only secondarily of the "mutual consolation of the spouses."

In the 19th and 20th centuries, however, the relationship of the spouses assumed new importance, as the church came to understand that marriage was a profoundly spiritual relationship in which partners experienced, through mutual affection and self-sacrifice, the unconditional love of God.

The Episcopal Church's 1979 *Book of Common Prayer* puts it this way: "We believe that the union of husband and wife, in heart, body and mind, is intended by God for their mutual joy; for the help and comfort given one another in prosperity and adversity; and, when it is God's will, for the procreation of children and their nurture in the knowledge and love of the Lord."

Broadening the Notion of Love

Our evolving understanding of what marriage is leads, of necessity, to a re-examination of who it is for. Most Christian denominations no longer teach that all sex acts must be open to the possibility of procreation, and therefore contraception is permitted. Nor do they hold that infertility precludes marriage. The church has deepened its understanding of the way in which faithful couples experience and embody the love of the creator for creation. In so doing, it has put itself in a position to consider whether same-sex couples should be allowed to marry.

Theologically, therefore, Christian support for same-sex marriage is not a dramatic break with tradition, but a recognition that the church's understanding of marriage has changed dramatically over 2,000 years.

I have been addressing the sound theological foundation for a new religious understanding of marriage, because it disturbs me greatly to see opposition to marriage for same-sex couples portrayed as the only genuinely religious or Christian position. I am somewhat awed by the breadth of religious belief and life experience reflected among more than 200 clergy colleagues who are publicly supporting marriage equality in D.C.

Avoiding Double Standards

But it's important to emphasize that the actions taken by the D.C. Council do not address the religious meaning of marriage at all. The proposed legislation would not force any congregation to change its religious teachings or bless any couple. Our current laws do not force any denomination to offer religious blessing to second marriages, yet those marriages, like interfaith marriages, are equal in the sight of the law even though some churches do not consider them religiously valid.

Existing laws require religious organizations that receive public funding to extend the same benefits to gay employees as to straight ones. In many instances, that includes health care for spouses. This has led some religious leaders, who believe same-sex marriage to be sinful, to threaten to get out of the social service business. I respect these individuals' right to their convictions, but I do not follow their logic. The Catholic

Church, for instance, teaches that remarriage without an annulment is sinful, yet it has not campaigned against extending health benefits to such couples. Additionally, several Catholic dioceses in states that permit same-sex marriage have found a way to accommodate themselves to such laws.

D.C.'s proposed marriage equality law explicitly protects the religious liberty of those who believe that God's love can be reflected in the loving commitment between two people of the same sex and of those who do not find God there. This is as it should be in a society so deeply rooted in the principles of religious freedom and equality under the law.

II

The battle over gay marriage has been waged for more than a decade, but within the last six months [of 2008]—since California legalized gay marriage and then, with a ballot initiative in November, amended its Constitution to prohibit it—the debate has grown into a full-scale war, with religious-rhetoric slinging to match. Not since 1860, when the country's pulpits were full of preachers pronouncing on slavery, pro and con, has one of our basic social (and economic) institutions been so subject to biblical scrutiny. But whereas in the Civil War the traditionalists had their [preacher and writer] James Henley Thornwell—and the advocates for change, their [clergyman and social reformer] Henry Ward Beecher—this time the sides are unevenly matched. All the religious rhetoric, it seems, has been on the side of the gay-marriage opponents, who use Scripture as the foundation for their objections.

The argument goes something like this statement, which the Rev. Richard A. Hunter, a United Methodist minister, gave to the *Atlanta Journal-Constitution* in June [2009]: "The Bible and Jesus define marriage as between one man and one woman. The church cannot condone or bless same-sex marriages because this stands in opposition to Scripture and our tradition."

To which there are two obvious responses: First, while the Bible and Jesus say many important things about love and family, neither explicitly defines marriage as between one man and one woman. And second, as the examples above illustrate, no sensible modern person wants marriage—theirs or anyone else's—to look in its particulars anything like what the Bible describes. "Marriage" in America refers to two separate things, a religious institution and a civil one, though it is most often enacted as a messy conflation of the two. As a civil institution, marriage offers practical benefits to both partners: contractual rights having to do with taxes; insurance; the care and custody of children; visitation rights; and inheritance. As a religious institution, marriage offers something else: a commitment of both partners before God to love, honor and cherish each other—in sickness and in health, for richer and poorer—in accordance with God's will. In a religious marriage, two people promise to take care of each other, profoundly, the way they believe God cares for them. Biblical literalists will disagree, but the Bible is a living document, powerful for more than 2,000 years because its truths speak to us even as we change through history. In that light, Scripture gives us no good reason why gays and lesbians should not be (civilly and religiously) married—and a number of excellent reasons why they should. . . .

Social conservatives point to Adam and Eve as evidence for their one man, one woman argument—in particular, this verse from Genesis: "Therefore shall a man leave his mother and father, and shall cleave unto his wife, and they shall be one flesh." But as Segal says, if you believe that the Bible was written by men and not handed down in its leather bindings by God, then that verse was written by people for whom polygamy was the way of the world. (The fact that homosexual couples cannot procreate has also been raised as a biblical objection, for didn't God say, "Be fruitful and multiply"? But the Bible authors could never have imagined the brave new world of international adoption and assisted reproductive technology—and besides, heterosexuals who are infertile or past the age of reproducing get married all the time.) . . .

The World Has Moved Forward

If the Bible doesn't give abundant examples of traditional marriage, then what are the gay-marriage opponents really exercised about? Well, homosexuality, of course—specifically sex between men. Sex between women has never, even in biblical times, raised as much ire. In its entry on "Homosexual Practices," the *Anchor Bible Dictionary* notes that nowhere in the Bible do its authors refer to sex between women, "possibly because it did not result in true physical 'union' (by male entry)." The Bible does condemn gay male sex in a handful of passages. Twice Leviticus refers to sex between men as "an abomination" (King James version), but these are throwaway lines in a peculiar text given over to codes for living in the ancient Jewish world, a text that devotes verse after verse to treatments for leprosy, cleanliness rituals for menstruating women and the correct way to sacrifice a goat—or a lamb or a turtle dove. Most of us no longer heed Leviticus on haircuts or blood sacrifices; our modern understanding of the world has surpassed its prescriptions. Why would we regard its condemnation of homosexuality with more seriousness than we regard its advice, which is far lengthier, on the best price to pay for a slave? . . .

Religious objections to gay marriage are rooted not in the Bible at all, then, but in custom and tradition (and, to talk turkey for a minute, a personal discomfort with gay sex that transcends theological argument). Common prayers and rituals reflect our common practice: the Episcopal *Book of Common Prayer* describes the participants in a marriage as "the man and the woman." But common practice changes—and for the better, as the Rev. Martin Luther King Jr. said, "The arc of history is long, but it bends toward justice." The Bible endorses slavery, a practice that Americans now universally consider shameful and barbaric. It recommends the death penalty for adulterers (and in Leviticus, for men who have sex with men, for that matter). It provides conceptual shelter for anti-Semites. A mature view of scriptural authority requires us, as we have in the past, to move beyond literalism. The Bible was written for a world so unlike our own, it's impossible to apply its rules, at face value, to ours.

Visions of Equal Unions

Marriage, specifically, has evolved so as to be unrecognizable to the wives of Abraham and Jacob. Monogamy became the norm in the Christian world in the sixth century; husbands' frequent enjoyment of mistresses and prostitutes became taboo by the beginning of the 20th. (In [a] *Newsweek* poll, 55 percent of respondents said that married heterosexuals who have sex with someone other than their spouses are more morally objectionable than a gay couple in a committed sexual relationship.) By the mid-19th century, U.S. courts were siding with wives who were the victims of domestic violence, and by the 1970s most states had gotten rid of their "head and master" laws, which gave husbands the right to decide where a family would live and whether a wife would be able to take a job. Today's vision of marriage as a union of equal partners, joined in a relationship both romantic and pragmatic, is, by very recent standards, radical, says Stephanie Coontz, author of "Marriage, a History." . . .

We cannot look to the Bible as a marriage manual, but we can read it for universal truths as we struggle toward a more just future. The Bible offers inspiration and warning on the subjects of love, marriage, family and community. It speaks eloquently of the crucial role of families in a fair society and the risks we incur to ourselves and our children should we cease trying to bind ourselves together in loving pairs. Gay men like to point to the story of passionate King David and his friend Jonathan, with whom he was "one spirit" and whom he "loved as he loved himself." Conservatives say this is a story about a platonic friendship, but it is also a story about two men who stand up for each other in turbulent times, through violent war and the disapproval of a powerful parent. David rends his clothes at Jonathan's death and, in grieving, writes a song:

I grieve for you, Jonathan my
brother;
You were very dear to me.
Your love for me was wonderful,
More wonderful than that of
women.

Here, the Bible praises enduring love between men. What Jonathan and David did or did not do in privacy is perhaps best left to history and our own imaginations.

In addition to its praise of friendship and its condemnation of divorce, the Bible gives many examples of marriages that defy convention yet benefit the greater community. The Torah discouraged the ancient Hebrews from marrying outside the tribe, yet Moses himself is married to a foreigner, Zipporah. Queen Esther is married to a non-Jew and, according to legend, saves the Jewish people. Rabbi Arthur Waskow, of the Shalom Center in Philadelphia, believes that Judaism thrives through diversity and inclusion. "I don't think Judaism should or ought to want to leave any portion of the human population outside the religious process," he says. "We should not want to leave [homosexuals] outside the sacred tent." The marriage of Joseph and Mary is also unorthodox (to say the least), a case of an unconventional arrangement accepted by society for the common good. The boy needed two human parents, after all.

The Message of Inclusion

In the Christian story, the message of acceptance for all is codified. Jesus reaches out to everyone, especially those on the margins, and brings the whole Christian community into his embrace. The Rev. James Martin, a Jesuit priest and author, cites the story of Jesus revealing himself to the woman at the well—no matter that she had five former husbands and a current boyfriend—as evidence of Christ's all-encompassing love. The great Bible scholar Walter Brueggemann, emeritus professor at Columbia Theological Seminary, quotes the apostle Paul when he looks for biblical support of gay marriage: "There is neither Greek nor Jew, slave nor free, male nor female, for you are all one in Jesus Christ." The religious argument for gay marriage, he adds, "is not generally made with reference to particular texts, but with the general conviction that the Bible is bent toward inclusiveness. . . ."

Still, very few Jewish or Christian denominations do officially endorse gay marriage, even in the states where it is legal. The practice varies by region, by church or synagogue, even by cleric. More progressive denominations—the United Church of Christ, for example—have agreed to support gay marriage. Other denominations and dioceses will do "holy union" or "blessing" ceremonies, but shy away from the word "marriage" because it is politically explosive. So the frustrating, semantic question remains: should gay people be married in the same, sacramental sense that straight people are? I would argue that they should. If we are all God's children, made in his likeness and image, then to deny access to any sacrament based on sexuality is exactly the same thing as denying it based on skin color—and no serious (or even semiserious) person would argue that. People get married "for their mutual joy," explains the Rev. Chloe Breyer, executive director of the Interfaith Center in New York, quoting the Episcopal marriage ceremony. That's what religious people do: care for each other in spite of difficulty, she adds. In marriage, couples grow closer to God: "Being with one another in community is how you love God. That's what marriage is about."

More basic than theology, though, is human need. We want, as Abraham did, to grow old surrounded by friends and family and to be buried at last peacefully among them. We want, as Jesus taught, to love one another for our own good— and, not to be too grandiose about it, for the good of the world. We want our children to grow up in stable homes. What happens in the bedroom, really, has nothing to do with any of this. . . .

> "Major religious denominations repre-
> senting millions of Americans ... sup-
> port the legal right to abortion."

Religious Americans Support Abortion Rights

Nancy Northup

Nancy Northup is the president of the Center for Reproductive Rights, a global human rights organization that uses constitutional and international law to secure women's reproductive freedom. In the viewpoint that follows, Northup claims that the U.S. Constitution guarantees personal liberty, including religious freedom and a woman's right to terminate an unwanted pregnancy. Northup argues that more Christians who value the separation of church and state should come forward to support reproductive rights because all rights in the United States are worth safeguarding. Without them liberty will cease to have meaning.

As you read, consider the following questions:

1. Which churches and religious branches support abortion rights, according to Northup?

Nancy Northup, "Because of, Not in Spite of, My Faith," RH Reality Check, October 14, 2008. www.rhrealitycheck.org, October 14, 2008. Reproduced by permission.

2. In the author's view, what is making the nation forget its commitment to religious freedom?

3. Why does Northup believe that those who are religious and support abortion rights often go unheard in reproductive rights debates?

I was born in the heartland—Kokomo, Indiana—and my family's eight moves took me to places as different as Temple, Texas, New York City, and a small town in [California's] Sacramento Valley. I sold Girl Scout cookies and earned merit badges. I marched down Main Street playing the flute in my green band uniform. I was co-captain of my cheerleading squad, pledged allegiance to the Flag, sang "God Bless America," and went to church on Sunday. I still go to church on Sunday. My religious faith informs everything that I do in my life, including my chosen work as an advocate for reproductive rights as a basic human right. I became a lawyer in large part because my faith called me to fight for social justice and the equality and dignity of all people.

Some people may be surprised that this bio belongs to such a visible and vocal voice for reproductive health. We're used to hearing such biographical attributes for those on the other side of the debate, but my Unitarian Universalist faith has long affirmed that laws that proscribe abortion are an affront to human life and dignity. We are not alone; major religious denominations representing millions of Americans (including the Episcopal Church, Presbyterian Church, United Methodist Church and Reform and Conservative branches of Judaism) support the legal right to abortion.

Safeguarding Personal Liberty

The attempt to legislate one set of religious beliefs about women's ability to control their reproductive lives is an offense to a bedrock commitment of America's constitutional democracy: freedom of religion and separation of church and state.

179

Not an Easy Choice

I never met a woman who made that decision [to end a pregnancy] lightly, without wrestling with the particularity of her own life situation and the effect her decision would have on others. Without considering whether she was ready and able to raise a child. Without agonizing over what is meant to terminate the life of a fetus with a serious genetic or developmental problem. Without examining her personal values in light of the values of her family, religion and society. . . . Yet in every situation I also witnessed the sense of relief and empowerment, personal growth and deepening ethical sense as each woman finally made and carried through on the decision that was best for her.

Barbara Gerlach, Religious Coalition for Reproductive Choice,
April 18, 2004. www.rcrc.org.

Yet growing fundamentalist influence over U.S. domestic and foreign policy is making the nation forget its commitment to religious freedom. This fundamentalist belief—that everyone must follow one set of religious truths—battles against a more open view that respects differences of religious beliefs and ethical positions.

It's human nature to want everyone to agree with one's religion or personal moral code. I understand that well. I taught Sunday school each week out of the desire to pass along my religious faith and traditions to the next generation. But I also accept that there will always be vast differences among religious and secular perspectives on life. And I understand, and firmly believe, that government should not help me or anyone else spread our religious beliefs. The government is not a Sunday school.

In *Roe v. Wade*, the Supreme Court grounded the right to privacy in the protection of personal liberty guaranteed by the Due Process Clause of the Fourteenth Amendment, and it recognized a notion of liberty that includes a woman's right to make fundamental decisions affecting her destiny, such as whether or not to terminate a pregnancy. Since then, the Court has recognized again and again that religion stands staunchly on both sides of the abortion issue, and that women and men of good conscience disagree about its moral implications. As the Supreme Court wrote in *Planned Parenthood v. Casey*, "reasonable people will have differences of opinion about these matters."

Because of, Not Despite, Faith

Given the different opinions that clearly exist on both sides, what I find most disturbing about the public debate on reproductive health, especially in an election year [2008], is that the moral case for reproductive decision-making isn't injected into the argument by those who support a woman's right to choose. While I've heard many politicians say that they are pro-choice *despite* their religious beliefs, I don't think I've heard anyone say that he or she supports reproductive health *because* of his or her faith. Perhaps it's because they feel those who oppose reproductive health have already claimed the moral stronghold, and that the public can't accept that there could be religious grounding on both sides of the debate.

As Americans we'll never agree on the validity of religious texts, but most of us agree that the Constitution is sacrosanct. Religious liberty is tied inextricably to Constitutional values. While the Constitution dictates that religion should not be legislated or imposed by government, it also allows that we should have the right of conscience in making personal decisions about when and whether to have a child. As Supreme Court Justice Anthony Kennedy wrote in *Casey*: "At the heart of liberty is the right to define one's own concept of existence, of meaning, of the universe, and of the mystery of human life." This is precisely why more of us should be talking about why our faith leads us to protect the health and lives of women and their families. We can't protect rights that we don't talk about.

| *"Christians are overwhelmingly pro-life."*

Religious Americans Do Not Support Abortion Rights

Dennis Di Mauro

In the following viewpoint, Dennis Di Mauro asserts that after the splintering of Christian churches in the 1960s on the issue of abortion, many formerly or predominantly pro-choice denominations are changing their official stance. According to Di Mauro, members of these congregations are battling with pro-choice factions to return their church's official position to a pro-life doctrine. Di Mauro believes that even if some churches still define themselves as pro-choice, most Christians are pro-life and should continue to advocate the sanctity of all life. Dennis Di Mauro is the secretary of the National Pro-Life Religious Council and the author of A Love for Life: Christianity's Consistent Protection of the Unborn.

As you read, consider the following questions:

1. As Di Mauro relates, what was the first Christian church to insist on the reformation of abortion laws in the 1960s?

Dennis Di Mauro, "Dubious Choice," *Touchstone: A Journal of Mere Christianity*, vol. 22, March 2009, pp. 39–41. Copyright © 2009 by the Fellowship of St. James. All rights reserved. Reproduced by permission.

2. According to the author, about what percent of the
   world's Christians worship in pro-life denominations
   (taking into account unaffiliated pro-life churches)?

3. What does Di Mauro say is regretfully the first reaction
   of most churches regarding the abortion issue?

The last decade [2000–2009] has seen a resurgence of interest in the abortion question. The passage of the Partial-
Birth Abortion Ban Act (including its successful review by the
Supreme Court in *Gonzalez v. Carhart*) and the public discussions of the gruesome nature of this type of abortion have
raised society's consciousness on the issue and have renewed a
national discussion on the sanctity of human life.

The high incidence of abortion in the United States, with
an estimated 1.2 million being performed every year, has also
raised concerns as to the wisdom of our current national
policy of abortion availability with few restrictions. Even many
social moderates have begun to question whether the legaliza-
tion of abortion, which was touted in the 1970s as a humane
way to handle crisis pregnancies (those resulting from rape or
incest, or involving fetal deformities or threats to the mother's
life), has become instead a vastly overused means of dealing
with any unwanted pregnancy.

Hot Debate Among Churches

Ethical questions on controversial issues have traditionally
come within the purview of the church, so the question of
abortion is one that has been hotly debated among the leaders
of nearly all Christian denominations in the United States.
These denominations have typically crafted written policy
statements regarding the morality of the procedure, which
have been approved at their denominational conventions
(usually held every three or four years).

The only exceptions to this pattern are those denominations with a non-centralized or congregational structure. These

church bodies are able to leave the question of whether abortion is ethical or not up to each local church congregation. An example of such a church body is the National Baptist Convention, the largest African American denomination in the United States, which has no written position on abortion.

But for the most part, policy positions have been completed, so that religious leaders can respond to their members' questions about abortion. The stances held by church bodies range from the strictly pro-life Roman Catholic Church to the strongly pro-choice United Church of Christ (UCC).

A denomination's position on the procedure is of vital importance, since it drives the church's activities in either a pro-life or pro-choice direction. For instance, a denomination with a pro-life statement is more likely to educate its members in a pro-life worldview, and to allow organizations, such as crisis pregnancy centers and denominational pro-life organizations (like Lutherans for Life, Presbyterians Pro-Life, and so forth) to give presentations and solicit funds at local parishes.

On the other hand, churches that have pro-choice statements are more likely to support such pro-abortion groups as the Religious Coalition for Reproductive Choice (RCRC), and also to include coverage for abortion in their church worker health insurance plans. Needless to say, the clergy in these denominations will also be much more likely to counsel a pregnant woman to have an abortion.

A Splintering in the 1960s

The disparity of views between denominations on the abortion question did not exist until the early 1960s. Before that time, all Christian denominations in the United States were pro-life.

But this changed in 1962, when the United Presbyterian Church, now part of the Presbyterian Church USA, called for the reform of abortion laws. The American Lutheran Church, now part of the Evangelical Lutheran Church of America

(ELCA), made a similar shift in teaching in 1963. During the late 1960s and early 1970s, nearly all the Protestant mainline denominations followed suit, including the American Baptist Church, the United Methodist Church, the United Church of Christ, and the Episcopal Church.

But despite the predominance of the pro-choice position in mainline Protestantism, a few pro-choice denominations have made significant comebacks towards a pro-life position since the late 1970s.

Southern Baptist Convention

The reversal of the Southern Baptist Convention's (SBC) position on abortion is the most radical reversal of abortion views of any major US church body. The SBC originally approved of the 1973 *Roe v. Wade* Supreme Court decision that legalized abortion in all fifty states, calling it an advance in the efforts for "religious liberty." During the following decade, the denomination was doctrinally polarized, with conservatives advocating adherence to biblical inerrancy, while moderates sought to maintain the inclusion of critical biblical scholarship within the denomination. But in 1979, the Southern Baptists elected a conservative slate of officers, and passed a resolution supporting the passage of the Human Life Amendment, a proposed amendment that would codify the right to life from the moment of conception into the US Constitution.

Today, the SBC is at the forefront of the pro-life movement, issuing numerous statements to educate its members and the public at large on the sanctity of life in the womb. One of the most outspoken Southern Baptists on the national stage has been Richard D. Land, the president of the denomination's Ethics and Religious Liberty Commission. Land has written extensively on the subject of abortion, defended the sanctity of life on his weekly radio programs, and actively lobbied Congress to enact pro-life laws. For example, he lobbied for the removal of abortion coverage from bills associated with the plans to institute a government-run national health care system in 1994.

The United Methodist Church

After the Southern Baptist Convention, the United Methodist Church (UMC) has probably made the greatest strides towards regaining a pro-life position. For instance, at its recent 2008 conference, the church added to its statement on abortion a clause concerning the necessity for its members to "respect . . . the sacredness of the life and well-being" of the unborn child, where previously it had only mentioned the "life and well being" of the mother. It also added the following sentence: "We support parental, guardian, or other responsible adult notification and consent before abortions can be performed on girls who have not yet reached the age of legal adulthood."

The denomination also stated that it "affirm[s] and encourage[s] the Church to assist the ministry of crisis pregnancy centers and pregnancy resource centers that compassionately help women find feasible alternatives to abortion." It also reduced previous callous language that described some crisis pregnancies as "unacceptable" to the mother.

Many of these changes can be attributed to the patient, long-term work of Lifewatch, also known as the Taskforce of United Methodists on Abortion and Sexuality (TUMAS). This organization has consistently preached about the sanctity of human life to a denomination that had essentially abandoned it.

This is not to say that the denomination is now fully pro-life, since its statement still includes the sentence, "We recognize tragic conflicts of life with life that may justify abortion, and in such cases we support the legal option of abortion under proper medical procedures," but its 2008 changes have made a difference in the way abortion is viewed.

The UMC also voted at the convention to maintain its membership in the Religious Coalition for Reproductive Choice (RCRC), but only by a 32-vote margin, the smallest in the denomination's history. And the vote was taken only after many of the more conservative African delegates to the convention had left. This is obviously encouraging, since it indicates the growth of pro-life sentiment within the denomination and signals the likelihood of further movement in the pro-life direction in the future.

The Presbyterian Church USA

As mentioned above, the United Presbyterian Church (UPC) began calling for the reform of abortion laws in 1962. In 1970, another Presbyterian denomination, the Presbyterian Church in the United States (PCUS) passed a statement at its convention liberalizing its views on abortion. In 1983, the PCUS and the UPC merged, forming the Presbyterian Church USA (PCUSA), and the new denomination's 1983 statement on abortion, was, according to former Presbyterians Pro-Life president, the Reverend Ben Sheldon, "the most radical [abortion] position of any U.S. denomination."

The consistent efforts of Presbyterians Pro-Life and other pro-life activists within the PCUSA have resulted in some small movements toward the pro-life position. For instance, at its General Assembly in 1997, the denomination included the following statement about the gruesome practice of partial-birth abortion: "The 209th General Assembly (1997) of the Presbyterian Church (U.S.A.) offer[s] a word of counsel to the church and our culture that the procedure known as intact dilation and extraction (commonly called 'partial-birth' abortion) of a baby who could live outside the womb is of grave moral concern and should be considered only if the mother's physical life is endangered by the pregnancy."

At its 2002 convention, the PCUSA also acknowledged that an abortion performed after fetal viability (the time when

A Compromise to Reduce Abortion

My humble, personal, non-kingdom, political proposal is that we might be able to move beyond the ugly impasse we've hit in our culture on the abortion issue—the impasse that is allowing babies to be aborted that *both sides* wish weren't aborted—by stretching our consensus on the "legal *loss* of personhood" to cover the "legal *beginning* of personhood." When the unborn's brainwaves are *above* the level that constitutes the loss of legal personhood, perhaps Americans could agree they should be considered legal persons. I am told by neurologists that this occurs between the 11th and 12th week of pregnancy.

With this compromise, Americans might be able to agree that all second and third trimester abortions should be outlawed. Moreover, with this compromise, Americans might be able to move beyond their polarized positions and rather work together to accomplish what the vast majority of Americans want: namely, a country in which abortions are as rare as possible and late-term abortions non-existent.

Gregory A. Boyd, Woodland Hills Church,
January 14, 2005. www.whchurch.org.

a child could be expected to survive outside the womb) "is a matter of grave moral concern," though it still claimed that such abortions were justified "in the rarest of circumstances and after prayer and/or pastoral care, when necessary to save the life of the woman, to preserve the woman's health in circumstances of a serious risk to the woman's health, to avoid fetal suffering as a result of untreatable life-threatening medical anomalies, or in cases of incest or rape."

Crunching the Numbers

These examples of trench battles between pro-choice and pro-life delegates at denominational conferences should not lead one to lose sight of the fact that Christian churches are still predominantly pro-life. Utilizing data from *The World Christian Encyclopedia* and *Adherents.com*, I performed a statistical analysis of the world's Christian denominations with respect to their position on abortion. Applying a methodology in which denominations whose position was unknown were categorized as pro-choice—that is, a methodology that would yield the most conservative estimate of pro-life denominations—I still found that 72 percent of the world's approximately two billion Christians worship in pro-life denominations.

Taking into consideration the large number of unaffiliated pro-life churches that exist in the world, it is highly likely that more than 75 percent of the world's Christian churches are pro-life, or, in other words, that pro-life churches outnumber pro-choice ones by at least a three-to-one margin. So the usual media message that gives the impression that Christians are evenly divided on the abortion issue is simply not true. The numbers reveal that Christians are overwhelmingly pro-life.

No Place for Abortion

Michael Gorman, author of *Abortion and the Early Church*, once told me that the Bible presents a worldview in which abortion simply has no place. It just doesn't fit in with the biblical stories. For instance, can we really imagine a woman in the first century walking up to Jesus, and after revealing her "unplanned" pregnancy to him, being given the equivalent of $300 by him and then advised to quickly have an abortion? Even though abortion was practiced in the first century, this scenario just doesn't fit the picture of how the Church was then or should be today.

Ultimately, the abortion question comes down to how the Church, as the Body of Christ, chooses to live. It seems that even in many of our Christian churches today, the first reaction is often to take the easy way out: to keep it quiet, and get rid of the problem. But this creates more problems than it solves: death for the unborn child, suffering and regret for the mother, and a betrayal of what it truly means to live in Christian love. Shouldn't each church congregation redouble its efforts in Christian charity to assist each mother to have her baby and raise that child to be a beloved disciple of Jesus?

Obviously, such a change in attitudes won't occur overnight in some churches, but pro-life position statements can help turn the tide against these tragic attitudes. Often, such changes can be started by a single church congregation, which can usually submit a pro-life statement for consideration at a denominational conference. Congregations can also encourage parish support of local crisis pregnancy centers, and can allow a foot in the door for organizations like Lifewatch and Presbyterians Pro-Life, who work so diligently to educate their fellow Christians on God's plan for human life. Efforts like these can affirm that a denomination's members are filled with God's love and the desire to nurture humanity's most vulnerable members.

> "Much of the debate over abortion is
> based on a misconception—that it is a
> religious issue."

Abortion Is Not a Religious Issue

Garry Wills

Garry Wills is the author of numerous books, most recently Head and Heart: American Christianities, *from which the following viewpoint is adapted. In it, Wills argues that abortion is not a religious issue because there is no specific biblical proclamation on the subject and religious philosophers have not traditionally defined abortion as an ecumenical concern. Wills claims that, instead, popes and religious thinkers have relegated abortion to the realm of reason and individual conscience. Wills supports this view, insisting that defining when a fetus gains personhood and determining who is permitted to make decisions concerning abortion are topics beyond the purview of religious leaders.*

As you read, consider the following questions:

1. What evidence does Wills provide to argue that the Catholic Church in the past did not treat abortion as murder?

Garry Wills, "Battling Abortions Isn't a Holy War," *Los Angeles Times*, November 4, 2007.
Copyright © 2007 Los Angeles Times. Reproduced by permission of the author.

2. According to the author, at what point in a fetus's evolution did Thomas Aquinas believe it gained a soul?

3. As Wills reports, what percent of abortions take place before the fetus possesses a functioning nervous system and cerebral cortex?

What makes opposition to abortion the issue it is for each of the GOP [Republican] presidential candidates is the fact that it is the ultimate "wedge issue"—it is nonnegotiable. The right-to-life people hold that it is as strong a point of religion as any can be. It is religious because the Sixth Commandment (or the Fifth by Catholic count) says, "Thou shalt not kill." For evangelical Christians, in general, abortion is murder. That is why what others think, what polls say, what looks practical does not matter for them. One must oppose murder, however much rancor or controversy may ensue.

Abortion Is Not Murder

But is abortion murder? Most people think not. Evangelicals may argue that most people in Germany thought it was all right to kill Jews. But the parallel is not valid. Killing Jews was killing persons. It is not demonstrable that killing fetuses is killing persons. Not even evangelicals act as if it were. If so, a woman seeking an abortion would be the most culpable person. She is killing her own child. But the evangelical community does not call for her execution.

About 10% of evangelicals, according to polls, allow for abortion in the case of rape or incest. But the circumstances of conception should not change the nature of the thing conceived. If it is a human person, killing it is punishing it for something it had nothing to do with. We do not kill people because they had a criminal parent.

Nor did the Catholic Church treat abortion as murder in the past. If it had, late-term abortions and miscarriages would have called for treatment of the well-formed fetus as a person, which would require baptism and a Christian burial. That was never the practice. And no wonder. The subject of abortion is not scriptural. For those who make it so central to religion, this seems an odd omission. Abortion is not treated in the Ten Commandments—or anywhere in Jewish Scripture. It is not treated in the Sermon on the Mount—or anywhere in the New Testament. It is not treated in the early creeds. It is not treated in the early ecumenical councils.

Lacking scriptural guidance, St. Thomas Aquinas worked from Aristotle's view of the different kinds of animation—the nutritive (vegetable) soul, the sensing (animal) soul and the intellectual soul. Some people used Aristotle to say that humans therefore have three souls. Others said that the intellectual soul is created by human semen.

Aquinas denied both positions. He said that a material cause (semen) cannot cause a spiritual product. The intellectual soul (personhood) is directly created by God "at the end of human generation." This intellectual soul supplants what had preceded it (nutritive and sensory animation). So Aquinas denied that personhood arose at fertilization by the semen. God directly infuses the soul at the completion of human formation.

Confounding the Evangelical View

Much of the debate over abortion is based on a misconception—that it is a religious issue, that the pro-life advocates are acting out of religious conviction. It is not a theological matter at all. There is no theological basis for defending or condemning abortion. Even popes have said that the question of abortion is a matter of natural law, to be decided by natural reason. Well, the pope is not the arbiter of natural law. Natural reason is.

John Henry Newman, a 19th century Anglican priest who converted to Catholicism, once wrote that "the pope, who comes of revelation, has no jurisdiction over nature." The

An Issue of Personal Morality

Before *Roe* [*v. Wade* Supreme Court decision], coura-
geous and compassionate clergy counseled millions of
women faced with unintended pregnancies and helped
them obtain abortions. More than thirty years ago, many
religious denominations passed resolutions in support of
women's right to legalized abortion. During the past
thirty-two years, our religious commitment to women's
right to abortion remains the same: women must be able
to make their own decisions based on their personal conscience and faith.

Debra W. Haffner,
Center for American Progress,
January 18, 2005. www.americanprogress.org.

matter must be decided by individual conscience, not by religious fiat. As Newman said: "I shall drink to the pope, if you
please—still, to conscience first, and to the pope afterward."

If we are to decide the matter of abortion by natural law,
that means we must turn to reason and science, the realm of
Enlightened religion. But that is just what evangelicals want to
avoid. Who are the relevant experts here? They are philosophers, neurobiologists, embryologists. Evangelicals want to ex-
clude them because most give answers they do not want to
hear. The experts have only secular expertise, not religious
conviction. They, admittedly, do not give one answer—they
differ among themselves, they are tentative, they qualify. They
do not have the certitude that the religious right accepts as
the sign of truth.

So evangelicals take shortcuts. They pin everything on being pro-life. But one cannot be indiscriminately pro-life.

If one claimed, in the manner of Albert Schweitzer, that all life deserved moral respect, then plants have rights, and it might turn out that we would have little if anything to eat. And if one were consistently pro-life, one would have to show moral respect for paramecia, insects, tissue excised during a medical operation, cancer cells, asparagus and so on. Harvesting carrots, on a consistent pro-life hypothesis, would constitute something of a massacre.

Opponents of abortion will say that they are defending only human life. It is certainly true that the fetus is human life. But so is the semen before it fertilizes; so is the ovum before it is fertilized. They are both human products, and both are living things. But not even evangelicals say that the destruction of one or the other would be murder.

Defenders of the fetus say that life begins only after the semen fertilizes the egg, producing an embryo. But, in fact, two-thirds of the embryos produced this way fail to live on because they do not embed in the womb wall. Nature is like fertilization clinics—it produces more embryos than are actually used. Are all the millions of embryos that fail to be embedded human persons?

The universal mandate to preserve "human life" makes no sense. My hair is human life—it is not canine hair, and it is living. It grows. When it grows too long, I have it cut. Is that aborting human life? The same with my growing human fingernails. An evangelical might respond that my hair does not have the potential to become a person. True. But semen has the potential to become a person, and we do not preserve every bit of semen that is ejaculated but never fertilizes an egg.

Defining Personhood

The question is not whether the fetus is human life but whether it is a human person, and when it becomes one. Is it when it is capable of thought, of speech, of recognizing itself as a person, or of assuming the responsibilities of a person? Is it when it has a functioning brain? Aquinas said that the fetus did not become a person until God infused the intellectual soul. A functioning brain is not present in the fetus until the end of the sixth month at the earliest.

Not surprisingly, that is the earliest point of viability, the time when a fetus can successfully survive outside the womb.

Whether through serendipity or through some sort of causal connection, it now seems that the onset of a functioning central nervous system with a functioning cerebral cortex and the onset of viability occur around the same time—the end of the second trimester, a time by which 99% of all abortions have already occurred.

Opponents of abortion like to show sonograms of the fetus reacting to stimuli. But all living cells have electric and automatic reactions. These are like the reactions of Terri Schiavo when she was in a permanent vegetative state.[1] Aquinas, following Aristotle, called the early stage of fetal development vegetative life. The fetus has a face long before it has a brain. It has animation before it has a command center to be aware of its movements or to experience any reaction as pain.

Partisan Politics

These are difficult matters, on which qualified people differ. It is not enough to say that whatever the woman wants should go. She has a responsibility to consider whether and when she may have a child inside her, not just a fetus. Certainly by the late stages of her pregnancy, a child is ready to respond with miraculous celerity to all the personal interchanges with the mother that show a brain in great working order.

Given these uncertainties, who is to make the individual decision to have an abortion? Religious leaders? They have no special authority in the matter, which is not subject to theo-

---

1. The case of Terry Schiavo, a woman who had been in a vegetative state for years, was the subject of a hot national debate in 2005 when her husband's request to have her life support discontinued was legally opposed by Terry's parents.

logical norms or guidance. The state? Its authority is given by the people it represents, and the people are divided on this. Doctors? They too differ. The woman is the one closest to the decision. Under *Roe vs. Wade*, no woman is forced to have an abortion. But those who have decided to have one are able to.

Some objected to [former deputy chief of staff to U.S. president George W. Bush] Karl Rove's use of abortion to cement his ecumenical coalition, on the grounds that this was injecting religion into politics. The supreme irony is that, properly understood, abortion is not even a religious issue. But that did not matter to Rove. All he cared about was that it worked. For a while.

| "A choice has to be made between Scripture, which is authored by God, and modern science, authored by men."

Belief in God and Evolution Are Incompatible

Andrew A. Snelling

Andrew A. Snelling insists in the following viewpoint that biblical history must be understood as world history if the Bible is God's word. Therefore, in Snelling's opinion, the book of Genesis defines the creation of the earth and its people. No evolutionary history existed before this time, Snelling contends, because genesis means "the beginning" and is the sole reliable account of the origins of the planet and the universe. Snelling maintains that Christians should accept these facts and not try to match misguided evolutionary thought with biblical truth. Andrew A. Snelling is a geologist and research scientist who lives and works in Australia. He serves as the director of research at Answers in Genesis, an organization that espouses creationism as historical fact.

Andrew A. Snelling, "Genesis: Real, Reliable, Historical," *Acts & Facts*, vol. 38, 2009, pp. 12–14. Copyright © 2009 Institute for Creation Research. All rights reserved. Reproduced by permission.

As you read, consider the following questions:

1. Why have many Christians "shelved" the apparent conflict between Genesis and evolutionary theory, according to Snelling?

2. Which of Adam's acts does the author believe illustrates his intellectual capacity, signaling that his descendents probably could have kept accurate records relating to creation?

3. As Snelling relates, which apostle prophesied that there would be scoffers who would "in the last days" choose to remain ignorant of the fact that God created the heaven and the earth?

The first eleven chapters of the Bible have been relegated by many to the category of myths, not real history. These are said to *contain* spiritual truth, but they cannot be taken seriously as records of real people and events. Many sincere Christians who believe the Bible do not know what their pastors believe about the historicity of Genesis. Is it safe to assume that these believe in the following truths?

1. God created everything in six 24-hour days.

2. Adam and Eve were real people.

3. God cursed a perfect world as a judgment for sin.

4. Noah constructed an Ark by which two of every kind of air-breathing, land-dwelling animal were saved along with Noah's family from a global flood.

5. The confusion of languages at the Tower of Babel produced the language groups that are found around the world today.

An alarming number of Christian leaders and teachers instead believe that God "created" through evolutionary processes over millions of years, that Adam and Eve descended from a hominid population, and that there has never been a global flood, suggesting that the account of Noah and the Ark is a story adapted from a Babylonian myth.

Mainstream Christian orthodoxy regarded the opening chapters of Genesis as just as real and reliable as the rest of the Bible until 150–2000 years ago. So what has happened?

This downgrading of the early chapters of Genesis has coincided with the rise of uniformitarian philosophy as the cornerstone of modern geology and of evolution as the core of modern biology. Christians have been ignorant of the process that has gradually changed their whole approach to the Bible. Consequently, Christian churches throughout the world reject the early chapters of Genesis as history, resulting in all manner of compromise intended to force geological ages and organic evolution into the Scriptures. Many Christians have shelved this apparent conflict as being divisive, too difficult to resolve, or irrelevant to the Christian faith.

Genesis as Reliable History

Yet the conflict still rages. What makes it more intense is that in the ranks of those Christians who have not compromised the historicity of Genesis are many scientists with doctoral degrees from the modern education system.

The Creation Science Movement in Great Britain and the Creation Research Society, which now boasts a membership of over 600 individuals with graduate degrees in science, have sought to remain faithful to accepting Genesis as reliable history. The Institute for Creation Research employed scientists with Ph.D.s to work full-time in creationist research, writing, and teaching. Other creationist groups were subsequently formed so that today there are creationist organizations in all corners of the globe.

So why would thousands of highly-trained scientists not only believe Genesis to be reliable history, but base their scientific research on the details and implications of that history? It stems foremost from their Christian convictions.

The Bible never claims to be a textbook on history or science, but if God is who He claims to be, then He has all knowledge and power, and never makes mistakes. Therefore, if the Bible is the Word of God, then it must be truthful, even when it touches upon matters of history and science. Otherwise, this Creator God is a liar. The very character of God requires the first eleven chapters of Genesis to be a trustworthy record.

The subsequent pages of Genesis recount the early history of the nation of Israel, beginning with Abraham. Few conservative Christian scholars would deny the historicity of these later chapters in Genesis. Yet many regard the creation account as a form of ancient Hebrew poetry, even though the genre throughout the first eleven chapters of Genesis is no different to that used in the remainder of the book. The conflict occurs not with the language but with the supposed scientific facts that insist on a multi-billion-year-old earth and organic evolution. A choice has to be made between Scripture, which is authored by God, and modern science, authored by men.

Liberal Christian scholars insist that Genesis was written perhaps as late as the post-Babylonian exile. But such claims overlook that in the pre-Flood world, people built cities, had tools of brass and iron, and made musical instruments. In Genesis 5, the record of Adam ends with the expression "this is the book of the generations of Adam." There is no reason to suppose that Adam and his descendants were not able to write and keep records, remembering that on the sixth day of creation Adam named all the animals, thus demonstrating his intellectual capacity.

Moses, the traditionally recognized author of Genesis, simply had to compile the book of Genesis from the records kept by Adam and his descendants. Thus Genesis reads as eyewitness accounts.

If the Creator God of the Bible is who He says He is, then not only is He capable of accurately telling us about the early universe, the earth, and man, but He is capable of having the details truthfully recorded and transmitted through successive generations.

Jesus and Genesis

If Jesus was (and is) both the Creator God and a perfect man, then His pronouncements are always and absolutely trustworthy. And Jesus referred directly to details in each of the first seven chapters of Genesis fifteen times. For example, Jesus referred to Genesis 1:26–97 when He said in Mark 10:6, "But from the beginning of the creation God made them male and female." Man was created male and female "from the beginning of the creation," not after millions of years. In the very next verse, Jesus quotes directly from Genesis 2:24 when He said, "For this cause shall a man leave his father and mother, and cleave to his wife; and they twain shall be one flesh." Five times Jesus refers to Noah and/or the destructive global Flood as real history. If He, as the Creator, was actually a witness to the events of Genesis 1–11, then we have no alternative but to regard these opening chapters of the Bible as reliable history.

The Apostle Peter's Prophecy

Peter spent three years traveling in the company of Jesus Christ Himself. Then Peter was a witness to Jesus' death and the bodily resurrection. Peter and the other disciples also received extraordinary ability and authority with the gift of God's Holy Spirit. Thus the books of the New Testament that bear his name not only come from his pen, but have the authority of God.

In 2 Peter 3:5–6, the apostle Peter prophesied that there would be scoffers who would come in the last days choosing to be ignorant of the fact that God created the heaven and the earth, and that God later destroyed everything on the surface of the earth by a global watery cataclysm.

Peter stated in 2 Peter 3:3, "knowing this first." This de-notes Peter placed first priority on this prophecy, which is about those who would reject the account of creation and the global Flood in Genesis 1–11 as real history.

What is quite remarkable is the explanation Peter gives as to why these scoff and reject the physical evidence that He created the heavens and the earth and sent a global mountain-covering flood. 2 Peter 3:4 tells that these scoffers' philosophy will be that "all things continue as they were from the begin-ning of the creation." This is an apt description of the phi-losophy of uniformitarianism, popularized by [geologist] Charles Lyell in the 1830s, that "the present is the key to the past." Thus we can extrapolate geological processes shaping the earth today back in time to explain how earth's rock fea-tures were formed.

It was on the basis of this philosophy that billions of years of slow and gradual geological processes became the founda-tion for modern geology. This provided the timescale neces-sary for the theory of organic evolution to explain the devel-opment of all life on the earth, instead of accepting that God had created it all.

Peter wrote an accurate description of these scoffers more than 1,700 years ago. Peter believed that the opening chapters of Genesis were real history and he predicted what we see to-day—the rejection of special creation by God and the rejec-tion of the global Flood.

Biblical Reliability

It is impossible to reject the historicity of the book of Genesis without repudiating the authority of the entire Bible. If Gen-esis is not true, then neither are the testimonies of those prophets and apostles who believed it was true. In the Old Testament, for example, Adam is mentioned in Deuteronomy, Job, and 1 Chronicles, while Noah is mentioned in 1 Chronicles, Isaiah, and Ezekiel. There are at least 100 quotations or direct references to Genesis 1–11 in the New Testament. Furthermore, every one of those eleven chapters is alluded to in the New Testament, and every one of the New Testament authors refers somewhere in his writings to Genesis 1–11.

In not one of these Old or New Testament references to Genesis is there the slightest evidence that the writers regarded the events as myths or allegories. The word *genesis* means "beginnings" or "origin," so Genesis 1–11 records for us God's provision of the only reliable account of the origin of the universe, the solar system, the earth, the atmosphere, and the oceans, of order and complexity, life, man, marriage, evil, language, government, culture, nations, and religion, not to mention rocks and fossils. Thus Genesis 1–11 is of such foundational importance to all history that without it there is no true understanding of ourselves or our world.

What we believe about our origin will inevitably determine our beliefs concerning our purpose and our destiny. Naturalistic concepts provide no hope of there being anything more than what we see around us. On the other hand, an origin at the hands of an all powerful, loving God guarantees a meaning to our existence, and a future. By not taking Genesis seriously, many Christians have in fact undermined the rest of the Bible they claim to believe and follow. They are also in danger of unwittingly accusing Jesus Christ of being a false witness, deceived, or a deceiver.

The Pivotal Importance of the Flood

The creation account in Genesis 1 is undoubtedly profound. However, the global Flood in Noah's day is of pivotal importance in understanding the present geology of the earth. Furthermore, more than any other branch of science, geology has been most affected by uniformitarianism. This philosophy and evolution have brought about rejection of Genesis 1–11, even by Christians. It is no wonder that the apostle Peter was led to single out those who reject the Genesis accounts. But God has also left in the rocks, fossils, and living world evidence that unmistakably testifies to the trustworthiness of the Genesis record. . . . The evidence we can observe today should be consistent with what we read in Genesis, because if it is God's Word, even details of science and history must be correct. . . . The Flood description implies catastrophism and utter devastation, and therefore we would expect the field data to be in harmony. The radioactive dating methods, geological processes, coal beds, oil, mineral deposits, and more can be seen only as perceived problems, not real ones.

> *"Most scientists who believe in God . . .*
> *find no contradiction between the sci-*
> *entific understanding of the world and*
> *the belief that God created that world."*

Belief in God and Evolution Are Not Incompatible

Karl Giberson and Darrel Falk

In the following viewpoint, Karl Giberson and Darrel Falk claim that belief in science and faith in the Christian religion are not incompatible. In their view, the Bible explains a moral code and not a history of creation. Giberson and Falk attest that evolutionary theory and the science of biology in general simply explain the wonders of living systems that God created and the manner in which the world changed over time as He intended. Karl Giberson is a professor at Eastern Nazarene College, copresident of the BioLogos Foundation, an organization that stresses harmony between science and faith. He is also the author of Saving Darwin: How to Be a Christian and Believe in Evolution. *Darrel Falk is a professor at Point Loma Nazarene University, copresident of the BioLogos Foundation, and the author of* Coming to Peace with Science: Bridging the Worlds Between Faith and Biology.

Karl Giberson and Darrel Falk, "We Believe in Evolution—and God," *USA Today,* August 10, 2009. Reproduced by permission of the authors.

As you read, consider the following questions:

1. According to a 2008 Gallup poll cited by the authors, what percent of Americans reject the theory of evolution?

2. As Giberson and Falk relate, how old is the earth according to young earth creationists?

3. Why is it significant that evolution is not "chaotic and wasteful," in Giberson and Falk's opinion?

The "conflict" between science and religion in America today is not only unfortunate, but unnecessary.

We are scientists, grateful for the freedom to earn Ph.D.s and become members of the scientific community. And we are religious believers, grateful for the freedom to celebrate our religion, without censorship. Like most scientists who believe in God, we find no contradiction between the scientific understanding of the world and the belief that God created that world. And that includes Charles Darwin's theory of evolution.

Many of our fellow Americans, however, don't quite see it this way, and this is where the real conflict seems to rest.

Creationism Shoehorning Science

Almost everyone in the scientific community, including its many religious believers, now accepts that life has evolved over the past 4 billion years. The concept unifies the entire science of biology. Evolution is as well-established within biology as heliocentricity is established within astronomy. So you would think that everyone would accept it. Alas, a 2008 Gallup Poll showed that 44% of Americans reject evolution, believing instead that "God created human beings pretty much in their present form at one time within the last 10,000 years."

The "science" undergirding this "young earth creationism" comes from a narrow, literalistic and relatively recent interpretation of Genesis, the first book in the Bible. This "science" is on display in the Creation Museum in Kentucky, where friendly dinosaurs—one with a saddle—cavort with humans in the Garden of Eden. Every week these ideas spread from pulpits and Sunday School classrooms across America. On weekdays, creationism is taught in fundamentalist Christian high schools and colleges. Science faculty at schools such as Bryan College in Tennessee and Liberty University in Virginia work on "models" to shoehorn the 15 billion year history of the universe into the past 10,000 years.

Evolution continues to disturb, threatening the faith of many in a deeply religious America, especially those who read the Bible as a scientific text. But it does not have to be this way.

Darwin's System

Such challenges to evolutionary science are paradoxical. Challenging accepted ideas is how America churns out Nobel Prize–winning science and patents that will drive tomorrow's technology. But challenging authority can also undermine this country's leadership in science, when citizens reject it.

Darwin proposed the theory of evolution in 1859 in *On the Origin of Species by Means of Natural Selection*. This controversial text presented evidence that present-day life forms have descended from common ancestors via natural selection. Organisms better adapted to their environments had more offspring, and these fitness adaptations accumulated across the millennia. And this is how new species arose.

In 1859 the evidence convinced many people, but not without challenges. Paleontology, the study of fossils, was new; no reliable way existed to determine the age of the Earth, and the physicists said it was too young to accommodate evolution, and Darwin knew nothing of genes, so the mechanism of inheritance—central to his theory—was shrouded in mystery.

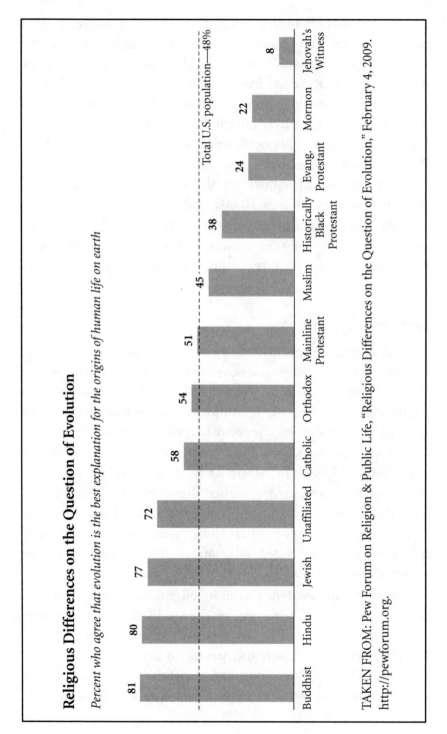

Religious Differences on the Question of Evolution

Percent who agree that evolution is the best explanation for the origins of human life on earth

Religion	Percent
Buddhist	81
Hindu	80
Jewish	77
Unaffiliated	72
Catholic	58
Orthodox	54
Mainline Protestant	51
Muslim	45
Historically Black Protestant	38
Evang. Protestant	24
Mormon	22
Jehovah's Witness	8

Total U.S. population—48%

TAKEN FROM: Pew Forum on Religion & Public Life, "Religious Differences on the Question of Evolution," February 4, 2009. http://pewforum.org.

But the biggest problem was dismay that humans were related to primates. "Descended from the apes? Dear me, let us hope it is not true," allegedly exclaimed the wife of a 19th-century English bishop upon hearing of Darwin's new theory. "But if it is true, let us hope it does not become widely known." Uneasy Christians hoped the advance of science would undermine Darwin's novel theory, which threatened their understanding of traditional biblical stories such as Adam and Eve, and the six days of creation.

In the years since Darwin argued natural selection was the agent of creation, the evidence for evolution has become overwhelming. The fossil record has provided evidence of compelling transitional species such as whales with feet. The discovery of DNA now provides an irrefutable digital record of the relatedness of all living things. And even the physicists have cooperated by proving that the Earth is 4.5 billion years old, providing plenty of time for evolution.

Evolution Is Not the Enemy

We are trained scientists who believe in God, but we also believe that science provides reliable information about nature. We don't view evolution as sinister and atheistic. We think it is simply God's way of creating. Yet we can still sleep soundly at night, with Bibles on our nightstands, resting atop the latest copy of *Scientific American*.

Are we crazy?

Evolution is not a chaotic and wasteful process, as the critics charge. Evolution occurs in an orderly universe, on a foundation of natural laws and faithful processes. The narrative of cosmic history preceding the origin of life is remarkable; the laws enabling life appear finely tuned for that possibility. The ability of organisms to evolve empowers them to adapt to changing environments. Our belief that God creates through evolution is a satisfying claim uniting our faith and our science. This is good news.

We have launched a website to spread this good news (www.biologos.org) and—we hope—to answer the many questions those of faith might have. BioLogos is a term coined by Francis Collins in his best seller *The Language of God: A Scientist Presents Evidence for Belief.* Collins, the Christian scientist who led the Human Genome Project, joined "bios," or life, with "logos," or word, from the first verse in the book of John in the New Testament.

The project aims to counter the voices coming from places such as the website Answers in Genesis, which touts creation scientists, and the Discovery Institute, a think tank in Seattle, that calls on Christians to essentially choose between science and faith.

We understand science as a gift from God to explore the creation, a companion revelation enriching the understanding of God we get from other sources, such as the Bible.

Many do not realize that making the Bible into a textbook of modern science is a recent development.

Many biblical scholars across the centuries have not seen it that way, concluding instead that the biblical creation story is a rich and complex text with many interpretations. Putting modern scientific ideas into this ancient story distorts the meaning of the text, which is clearly about God's faithful and caring relation to the world, not the details of how that world came to be.

What we learn from science cannot threaten our belief in God as the creator if God created the universe in a Big Bang 15 billion years ago, guided its development with elegant mathematical laws so that eventually there would be big-brained mammals exploring things such as beauty, morality and truth, than let us celebrate that idea, not reject it.

Periodical Bibliography

The following articles have been selected to supplement the diverse views presented in this chapter.

Hadley Arkes   "Empathy and Apathy," *First Things*, August/September 2009.

David Boies   "Gay Marriage and the Constitution," *Wall Street Journal*, July 20, 2009.

Owen F. Campion   "A Question of Witness to the Church," *Priest*, March 2010.

Mary Eberstadt   "Pro-animal, Pro-life," *First Things*, June/July 2009.

Anthony Esolen   "Married with Reservations," *Touchstone*, September/October 2009.

John Garvey   "Magical Thinking," *Commonweal*, January 30, 2009.

Andrew Harmon   "Reduce, Reuse, Religion?" *Advocate*, May 2009.

Damien Marie Savino   "Atheistic Science: The Only Option?" *Logos*, Fall 2009.

Thomas A. Shannon   "A Change in Tone," *Catholic New Times*, February 16, 2009.

Tome Suozzi   "Why I Now Support Gay Marriage," *New York Times*, June 12, 2009.

For Further Discussion

Chapter 1

1. In the first two viewpoints, both M. Stanton Evans and Jack Feerick attempt to define the impact of religion on the Founding Fathers during the formative years of the United States. Conduct some additional research into the beliefs of these men and determine which viewpoint you find more credible. Do you believe that Evans presents a more accurate reading of history when he argues that the Founders felt religion was an important part of U.S. society? Or do you think Feerick's historical analysis is more accurate in its conclusion that the Founders had a secular vision for the country? Use quotes from both viewpoints and your additional sources to support your conclusion.

2. Viewpoints 3 and 4 in the first chapter assess the state of Christianity in contemporary U.S. society. Barry A. Kosmin and Ariela Keysar present findings of the American Religious Identification Survey and come to the conclusion that the United States is becoming a less Christian nation. Ed Stetzer analyzes statistics from that same survey and others but comes to a different conclusion, contending that the country is not becoming less Christian, just changing its definition of Christianity. Which viewpoint more accurately assesses the statistics? What leads you to believe one author's analysis over the other? Be specific in your explanation.

Chapter 2

1. Both authors of the first two viewpoints in chapter 2 cite numerous statistics and studies in making their claims that religion benefits or harms society. How does this use

of statistics make you feel about the authors' assertions? Do statistics necessarily validate an argument? Is one author's use of studies and statistics more convincing than the other's? Include examples from the viewpoints to back up your claims.

2. In viewpoint 3 in chapter 2, Aimee Welch outlines the benefits of the faith-based program Faith Works as a tool to help strengthen U.S. society, and in viewpoint 4, Barry Lynn critiques the government's implementation of these programs. Reread both viewpoints and decide whether you think faith-based programs have an important role to play in American society. Can faith-based programs fill in gaps where government cannot reach the people most in need? Should the government ever give money to a religious organization, regardless of its motivations and the guidelines implemented to ensure the separation of church and state? Why or why not?

3. After reading the final viewpoints in chapter 2, do you believe it is possible to separate religion and politics in the United States? Think back to the 2008 elections and the candidates' mentions of religion. Did you think their discussion of personal religious beliefs seemed genuine, or do you think that it is too much to ask of politicians to honestly discuss this topic? Do you think that religion has an important function in American public life, as contended by Hunter R. Rawlings III, or should it be left out of politics entirely? Or do you believe, as suggested by Jon Meacham, that the Founding Fathers wanted to create a culture in which the secular and religious could coexist? Do you think religion plays a role in your decision to vote for a candidate? Explain why or why not.

Chapter 3

1. The articles by William R. Mattox Jr. and Michael Jinkins contest the notion of teaching the Bible in public schools.

Mattox's claim rests on the presumption that all students benefit from an understanding of Bible stories and characters because these narratives are part of the foundation of Western thought and greatly impact philosophy and literature. Do you believe that Bible classes could be taught successfully in a secular setting? What would be the obstacles to making such classes work? Draw arguments from the two aforementioned articles when drafting your response.

2. The pair of articles on medical practitioners potentially denying services to patients because of the practitioners' religious beliefs debate an issue concerning individual rights. Either the physician's right to refuse service or the patient's right to receive medical help must seemingly win out in this contest. Whose rights do you think should ultimately decide this controversy? Or can you conceive of a solution that would respect both doctor and patient rights? Explain your answer.

3. After rereading the articles by Ron Johnson Jr. and Eric Williams, explain whether you think the 1954 tax law that prohibits church leaders from endorsing political candidates is fair and just. In answering this question, be sure to seek out the wording of the law and consider Johnson's argument that preachers had traditionally spoken out in favor of political candidates throughout the early part of American history.

Chapter 4

1. After examining the first two viewpoints in this chapter, explain what kinds of arguments Mark Galli, John Bryson Chane, and Lisa Miller make in their case for or against the acceptance of same-sex marriage in the Christian Church. What moral arguments underpin their contentions? Cite examples to illustrate your assessment.

2. Nancy Northup makes the argument that Christians in the United States should support abortion rights because in her view safeguarding personal liberty is the issue's central concern. In her view, all Americans enjoy their freedoms because the separation of church and state ensures that no one group, religion, or ideology can dictate morality. Dennis Di Mauro, however, believes that churches in America have a duty to declare their opposition to "tragic attitudes" that cheapen life and lead the country away from religious values. Do you believe the separation of church and state should define the United States' response to moral issues or are there some instances in which religious ethics should decide the outcome of these controversies? Explain why or why not. Be sure to examine the potential pitfalls or shortcomings of embracing either position.

3. The final pair of viewpoints in the fourth chapter debate the question of whether science and religion can collaborate in explaining the planet's evolution. Using the arguments put forth by Andrew A. Snelling, Karl Giberson, and Darrel Falk, explain what is at stake in this debate. That is, what do the authors believe will be sacrificed if their view is ignored or even contested? Draw quotes from the articles in making your assessment.

Organizations to Contact

The editors have compiled the following list of organizations concerned with the issues debated in this book. The descriptions are derived from materials provided by the organizations. All have publications or information available for interested readers. The list was compiled on the date of publication of the present volume; the information provided here may change. Be aware that many organizations take several weeks or longer to respond to inquiries, so allow as much time as possible.

American Atheists
PO Box 158, Cranford, NJ 07016
(908) 276-7300 • fax: (908) 276-7402
Web site: www.atheists.org

American Atheists was founded in 1963 and has since been the nation's most active organization working to protect the civil liberties of atheists in the United States and to ensure the complete separation of church and state. Through its demonstrations and conventions, outreach and education, and publications the organization has sought to foster a broader understanding of atheism and protect atheists' right to not believe. Information about the intrusion of religion into politics and the military can be found on the American Atheists Web site.

American Civil Liberties Union (ACLU)
125 Broad St., 18th Floor, New York, NY 10004
(212) 607-3300 • fax: (212) 607-3318
Web site: www.aclu.org

The ACLU is dedicated to protecting the civil liberties guaranteed to all Americans by the Bill of Rights and the Constitution. Through its educational programs, outreach, legal efforts, and publications, the ACLU actively works to ensure Americans' constitutional rights are not ignored. With regard to religion, the organization believes that the right to practice, or not practice, religion is fundamental to the freedom of the country. The ACLU addresses issues including the free exercise of religion, government-funded religion, and religion in schools. Information on these topics and others can be found on the ACLU Web site.

Americans United for Separation of Church and State (AU)

518 C Street NE, Washington, DC   20002
(202) 466-3234 • fax: (202) 466-2587
e-mail: americansunited@au.org
Web site: www.au.org

Since 1947, AU has been working to ensure separation of church and state and religious freedom for all Americans. A nonpartisan organization, AU tackles a wide range of issues in its publications and activism, including church politicking, "faith-based" initiatives, freedom of religion, marriage and sexuality, and religion and education. The organization's Web site is organized by issue and offers detailed and up-to-date information on each topic. *Church & State* is the organization's monthly publication.

Christianity Today International (CTI)

465 Gundersen Drive, Carol Stream, IL   60188
(630) 260-6200 • fax: (630) 260-0114
Web site: www.christianitytoday.com

CTI is a not-for-profit communications ministry founded by internationally known Christian evangelist Billy Graham. The organization seeks to promote a Christian worldview through the publication of eleven magazines designed for both Christian leadership and the general public. *Christianity Today* is the monthly flagship publication of CTI with the other magazines focusing on specific groups such as college students and men. Articles from many of these publications can be accessed online.

Council for Secular Humanism

PO Box 664, Amherst, NY   14226-0664
(716) 636-7571 • fax: (716) 636-1733
e-mail: info@secularhumanism.org
Web site: www.secularhumanism.org

The Council for Secular Humanism advocates for and defends a nonreligious worldview based on science, naturalistic philosophy, and humanist ethics. Rejecting supernatural and authoritarian beliefs, secular humanists value reason and scientific inquiry, individual freedom, human values, and tolerance. In accordance with these beliefs, the council seeks to ensure the separation of church and state in U.S. society. The council's Web site provides information about secular humanism and a selection of articles from *Free Inquiry*, the organization's bimonthly magazine.

Focus on the Family

Colorado Springs, CO   80995
(800) 232-6459
Web site: www.focusonthefamily.com

Focus on the Family is a Christian organization dedicated to promoting traditional family values rooted in the Christian faith. Through its outreach programs, publications, broadcasts, and interactive forums, the organization seeks to advance beliefs such as a traditional definition of marriage and the sanctity of life. Additional information on these topics and others can be found on the Focus on the Family Web site.

Interfaith Alliance

1212 New York Ave. NW, Suite 1250, Washington, DC   20005
(202) 238-3300 • fax: (202) 238-3301
Web site: www.interfaithalliance.org

The Interfaith Alliance seeks to protect both democracy and religion in America by promoting government policies that preserve the separation of church and state, organizing grassroots activism, aiding politicians in observing the boundaries of church and state during elections, and educating the public in order to increase respect for and understanding of different religions. The organization publishes an online newsletter that is sent to all members of the organization, and its Web site provides a "Media Roundup" that offers information about the role religion has played in recent political campaigns.

Muslim American Society (MAS)
PO Box 1896, Falls Church, VA 22041
(703) 998-6525 • fax: (703) 998-6526
e-mail: mas@masnet.org
Web site: www.masnet.org

MAS is an organization combining charitable works with religious, social, cultural, and educational activities in an effort to promote Islam and increase understanding of the religion within U.S. society at large. Articles such as "Islamic Community in North America: Prospects and Problems" and "Mainstream Islam in the African-American Experience," present information about the role of Islam in American society. Additional articles categorized under headings such as contemporary issues, Islamic sciences, and history and civilization can be read on the MAS Web site.

National Association of Evangelicals (NAE)
PO Box 23269, Washington, DC 20026
(202) 789-1011 • fax: (202) 842-0392
Web site: www.nae.net

NAE represents American evangelicals and the forty-five thousand local churches they attend across the United States. The organization seeks to extend the kingdom of God through church partnerships, political work, its chaplains commission, and the provision of world relief. Information about current activities can be read on the NAE Web site along with publications such as "For the Health of the Nation," a document guiding NAE political action within seven different issues, including religious freedom, the sanctity of life, and human rights.

Secular Coalition for America
PO Box 66096, Washington, DC   20035-6096
(202) 299-1091
Web site: www.secular.org

The Secular Coalition for America conducts advocacy work on behalf of its member organizations with nonreligious founding principles. It lobbies Congress directly on issues such as religious discrimination in the military, religious control of sex education, and religious refusal laws affecting emergency contraception access. Overviews and position papers of these issues and others can be read on the coalition's Web site.

Sojourners
3333 Fourteenth Street NW, Suite 200
Washington, DC   20010
(202) 328-8842 • fax: (202) 328-8757
e-mail: sojourners@sojo.net
Web site: www.sojo.net

Sojourners was founded in 1971 with the goal of elucidating the connection between the Bible and social justice, spreading hope, and, through its actions, impressing positive change on individual, local, national, and international levels. While Sojourners presents religious viewpoints on societal issues such as abortion, homosexuality, education, and the role of government, among others, there is an emphasis on understanding and tolerance running throughout the discussion of these topics. *Sojourners* magazine is published monthly, further expanding on these subjects and others.

Vision America
PO Box 10, Lufkin, TX   75902
(866) 522-5582 • fax: (936) 560-3902
e-mail: mail@visionamerica.us
Web site: www.visionamerica.us

Vision America works to aid pastors in their efforts to restore Judeo-Christian values as the foundation of U.S. society and to increase civic involvement. The organization promotes ideals such as the sanctity of human life, marriage, and family; personal decency and moral integrity; and religious liberty. Audio recordings of founder Rick Scarborough's sermons can be listened to online or downloaded, and the "Scarborough Report" presents the founder's musings on current religiously centered issues in the United States.

Bibliography of Books

Richard Alba, Albert J. Raboteau, and Josh DeWind, eds.
Immigration and Religion in America: Comparative and Historical Perspectives. New York: New York University Press, 2009.

Brooke Allen
Moral Minority: Our Skeptical Founding Fathers. Chicago: Ivan R. Dee, 2006.

Chas S. Clifton
Her Hidden Children: The Rise of Wicca and Paganism in America. Lanham, MD: AltaMira, 2006.

Joan DelFattore
The Fourth R: Conflicts over Religion in America's Public Schools. New Haven, CT: Yale University Press, 2004.

David Domke and Kevin Coe
The God Strategy: How Religion Became a Political Weapon in America. New York: Oxford University Press, 2008.

Marie A. Eisenstein
Religion and the Politics of Tolerance: How Christianity Builds Democracy. Waco, TX: Baylor University Press, 2008.

David Hillel Gelernter
Americanism: The Fourth Great Western Religion. New York: Doubleday, 2007.

Steven Goldberg   *Bleached Faith: The Tragic Cost When Religion Is Forced into the Public Square.* Stanford, CA: Stanford Law Books, 2008.

Richard Grigg   *Beyond the God Delusion: How Radical Theology Harmonizes Science and Religion.* Minneapolis: Fortress, 2008.

Timothy L. Hall   *American Experience: Religion in America.* New York: Facts On File, 2007.

Peter Herriot   *Religious Fundamentalism: Global, Local and Personal.* New York: Routledge, 2009.

Phillip Jenkins   *Dream Catchers: How Mainstream America Discovered Native Spirituality.* New York: Oxford University Press, 2005.

Steven L. Jones   *Religious Schooling in America: Private Education and Public Life.* Westport, CT: Praeger, 2008.

Karen Judson   *Religion and Government: Should They Mix?* New York: Benchmark, 2009.

Frank Lambert   *Religion in American Politics: A Short History.* Princeton, NJ: Princeton University Press, 2008.

William Lobdell	*Losing My Religion: How I Lost My Faith Reporting on Religion in America—and Found Unexpected Peace.* New York: HarperCollins, 2009.
Robert S. McElvaine	*Grand Theft Jesus: The Hijacking of Religion in America.* New York: Three Rivers Press, 2009.
Sallie McFague	*A New Climate for Theology: God, the World and Global Warming.* Minneapolis: Fortress, 2008.
Chris Mooney and Sheril Kirs	*Unscientific America: How Scientific Illiteracy Threatens Our Future.* New York: Basic Books, 2009.
Geiko Müller-Fahrenholz	*America's Battle for God: A European Christian Looks at Civil Religion.* Grand Rapids, MI: William B. Eerdmans, 2007.
Fred Nadis	*Wonder Shows: Performing Science, Magic, and Religion in America.* Piscataway, NJ: Rutgers University Press, 2005.
Robert H. Nelson	*The New Holy Wars: Economic Religion vs. Environmental Religion in Contemporary America.* University Park: Pennsylvania State University Press, 2010.
Mark A. Noll	*God and Race in American Politics: A Short History.* Princeton, NJ: Princeton University Press, 2008.

Joseph L. Price | *Rounding the Bases: Baseball and Religion in America.* Macon, GA: Mercer University Press, 2006.

Richard W. Santana | *Religion and Popular Culture: Rescripting the Sacred.* Jefferson, NC: McFarland, 2008.

Jeffrey S. Siker, ed. | *Homosexuality and Religion: An Encyclopedia.* Westport, CT: Greenwood, 2007.

Robert Murray Thomas | *God in the Classroom: Religion and America's Public Schools.* Westport, CT: Praeger, 2007.

Hugh B. Urban | *The Secrets of the Kingdom: Religion and Concealment in the Bush Administration.* Lanham, MD: Rowman and Littlefield, 2007.

Index

Solzhenitsyn, Aleksandr, 166
Somerville, Margaret, 162–163
Souter, David, 25
Southern Baptist Convention
(SBC), 186–187
Southern Baptist Theological
Seminary, 15
Southern religious principles,
31–32
Stanley, Erik, 146
Stark, Rodney, 59
Stem cell research, 107, 109, 129–
130
Stetson, Chuck, 120
Stetzer, Ed, 53–62
Stormans Inc. v. Selecky, 131–132
Strong, Caleb, 29
Suicide, 76, 81, 85–86, 129
Sullivan, Andrew, 161
Supreme Court, 41, 181

T

Taskforce of United Methodists on
Abortion and Sexuality
(TUMAS), 187
Tax-exempt status, 150–151
Tax money, 27, 29, 37, 98–99
Teen Challenge (drug addiction
program), 73–74
Teen pregnancy, 85
Ten Commandments, 36
Terrorism, 41, 154
Theological polarization, 50–51
Thornwell, James Henley, 171
Torah, 175
Treaty of Tripoli, 104

U

Union of Orthodox Jewish Con-
gregations, 97
Unitarianism, 32, 140, 179
United Church of Christ (UCC),
176, 185
United Methodist Church (UMC),
49, 187–188
United Presbyterian Church. *See*
Presbyterians
USA Today (newspaper), 57

W

Wachlin, Marie, 120
Waggoner, Brad, 60
War of Independence, 26–27
Warren, Rick, 158
Washington, George, 26–27, 30,
78, 103, 104
Washington Post (newspaper), 54,
57
Waskow, Arthur, 175
Welch, Aimee, 87–93
White, A.D., 107
Wiccanism, 57
Wilcox, W. Bradford, 71
Williams, Eric, 147–151
Williams, Roger, 104
Williamson, Hugh, 32
Wills, Garry, 192–198
Wilson, James, 31
Witherspoon, John, 28
Wolpe, David, 16, 17
World Vision, 97, 99